EXECUTIVE
PLANNING
WITH BASIC

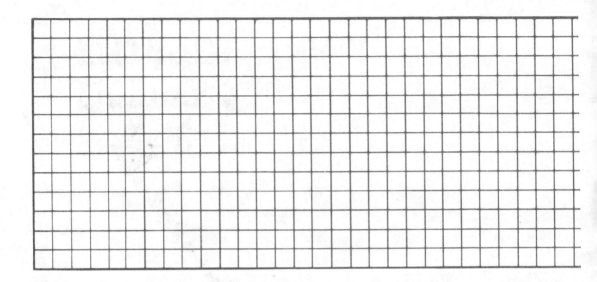

EXECUTIVE PLANNING WITH BASIC

X.T. BUI

Berkeley • Paris • Düsseldorf

CREDITS
English version by Douglas Hergert
Applesoft version of BASIC programs by Douglas Hergert
Cover Art by Vincent Chaix
Book composition and technical illustrations by Judy L. Wohlfrom

Library of Congress Card Number: 81-85954
ISBN 0-89588-083-0
Printed in the United States of America
1 2 3 4 5 6 7 8 9 10

To my parents

TABLE OF CONTENTS

ACKNOWLEDGEMENTS

The author would like to thank Jacques Pasquier, dean of the Faculty of Law and Economic and Social Sciences of Fribourg University, and professor of business economics and finance at Fribourg and Lausanne Universities, for his constant support and encouragement. Thanks also go to Jean-Marie Jacazio for his valuable suggestions; Mark Mauron for materials he supplied during the preparation of this book; and Douglas Hergert for many useful suggestions.

INTRODUCTION

Executive Planning with BASIC is a collection of interactive, business-oriented programs in BASIC; they can all be used in their present form as tools for management and planning decisions. Thorough discussions of the background and development of each tool, and application examples from actual business sources will help you understand the methods described in each chapter.

The book has three goals:

1. To explain the quantitative methods of management decision-making in clear and practical terms.

2. To dispel the idea, common in commercial and financial circles, that programming is only for specialists. Thanks to BASIC, it is practical for management to have direct access to computers for analysis, planning, and control. Experience has shown the benefits that result from personal exposure to the power of a computer in the various areas of management.

3. To provide an efficient and time-saving set of computer implementations for quantitative analysis; since the problems of management decision-making are becoming more and more complex, managers must now devote their personal resources to analysis, reflection, and judgment rather than to the development of accounting tools.

This book is designed to serve both as a teaching text and as a reference work for professionals in the field. It will help data processing professionals, economists, and managers to understand the techniques of data processing for management decisions. This understanding will lead to better decision-making and improved general performance.

The programs of this book are organized into the following five groups:

- Decision Models under Certainty
- Decision Models under Uncertainty
- Forecasting Models
- Investment Models
- Multicriteria Decision-Aid Model.

Three appendices complete the text:

- Statistical Analysis Programs
- Matrix Operation Subroutines
- A Summary of BASIC.

Each chapter contains five sections:

1. *A concise description of the method to be examined:* definitions, fundamental principles, application areas.
2. *A description of the program:* its structure, its characteristics, and the options it offers to the user.
3. *An application example,* illustrating how the program can be used.
4. *The output from a run* of the program, using the data from the application example described above.
5. *A complete listing* of the program.

The BASIC computer language is easy to learn and to use. The essentials of BASIC are expressed in twenty or so simple instruction words (such as **READ, PRINT, FOR/TO/NEXT, IF/THEN**, and so on). BASIC is thus an excellent language for those who wish to solve information problems with a computer, without devoting excessive time and effort to the technicalities of software systems.

This book may be used either by the manager who needs an immediate implementation of the powerful techniques described, or by the data processing professional whose interest in programming may lead to an in-depth examination of the structure of each program presented.

A business manager begins by formulating a question or a problem to be solved and then chooses the model that most closely fits this formulation. The format of this book will guide the decision-maker in both of these tasks; particularly relevant are the descriptions of the models, and the application examples, which clarify the use of each program.

For the programmer who might be assigned the task of modifying these programs according to a given set of specifications, the structure of each program has been carefully outlined and the essential algorithms have been described. Many of the programs in this book can easily be abridged to perform a very specific task or generalized to take on a broader family of tasks. For example, the Multiple Linear Regression program can be "down-graded" for use with a fixed number of dependent variables. On the other hand, the Portfolio Management Program can be "up-graded" for input of covariances.

All the programs in this book have been run and tested on the Apple II computer, and on the Ohio Scientific C-1P and C-4P microcomputers. Some of the programs have also been tested on Commodore's CBM 3032 and the P-2000 from Philips. While there are some implementation differences between BASICs, adapting these programs to different computers should be an easy task.

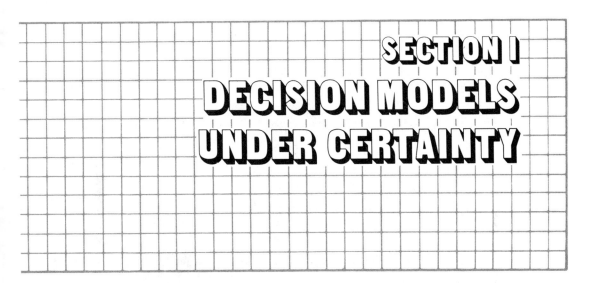

SECTION I
DECISION MODELS UNDER CERTAINTY

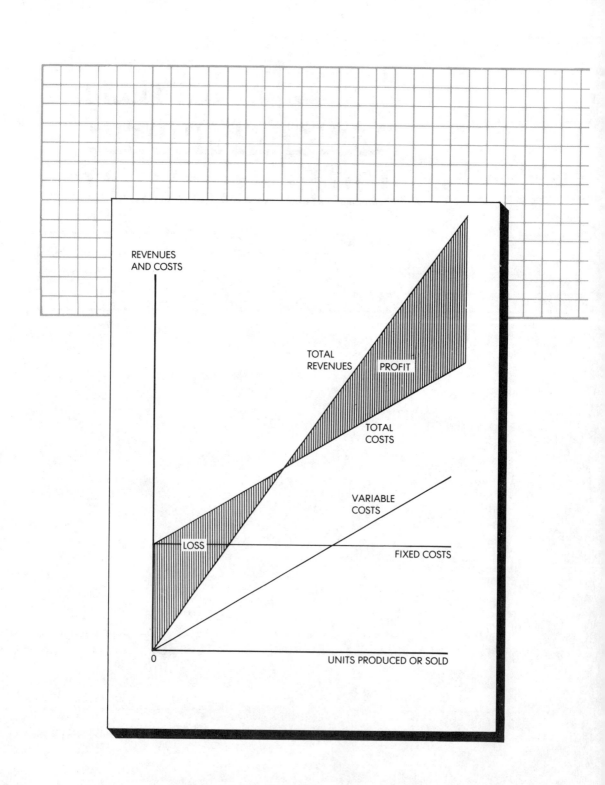

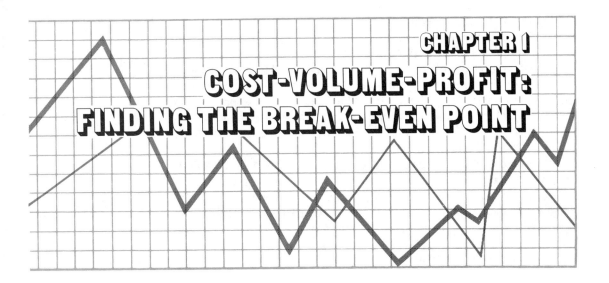

CHAPTER I
COST-VOLUME-PROFIT:
FINDING THE BREAK-EVEN POINT

THE METHOD

Break-even point analysis is a management financial tool that supplies a clear picture of the relationship between fixed costs, variable costs, and the potential profits from an investment project. Break-even point analysis indicates the level of production at which the income from sales exactly covers the total production costs.

The calculation of the break-even point is characterized by the fact that some costs are fixed and others are variable; a company must operate at a loss until a certain level of production (and thus of sales) is achieved. The break-even point can be defined as the cost-volume-profit ratio giving both a profit and a loss of zero.

THE PROGRAM

The break-even point program offers the user two different calculation options. The first, based on the *maximum production capacity,* is used for a specific product or for a specific production department. The second, based on sales, might generally be applied to all the activities of the company.

The advantage of the second method over the first is that it allows calculation of a break-even point for an entire organization that sells several products at different prices.

The first method is implemented in program lines 190 to 300 and 430 to 530. The break-even point formula is defined in line 220. Since the business manager is, in principle, free to determine the production volume (which might well vary from zero to the maximum capacity), it is useful to know how the profit changes for different levels of production. Lines 470 to 520 create a tabular presentation of this function.

Lines 310 to 410 calculate the break-even point for the second method. Line 340 contains the basic formula. Since this method is based on sales forecasts, the program also derives the expected profit (lines 390 to 410).

The program also performs some simple error checking. Line 140 reminds the user that the selling price of a product must be greater than its variable cost per unit. Lines 230 and 350 check that the input data do not conflict with the break-even point model.

APPLICATION EXAMPLE

The Problem

Jones, Inc., is a medium-sized company. In order to decrease production bottle-necks, the company is considering the purchase of an additional assembly machine. With the new machine, the variable costs per unit will be decreased by 25%, specifically due to a reduction in turn-around time. The new machine will *increase* the total fixed costs by $1500. Supposing that no other cost elements enter into the analysis, Jones wants to find out whether or not the new machine will be an advantage.

The Data

The following table summarizes the cost, sales, and production data for Jones, Inc.:

	Before Purchase of Second Machine	After Purchase of Second Machine
Total fixed costs	3000	4500
Variable costs per unit	10	7.50
Unit sales price	20	20
Expected unit sales	500	500
Maximum production capacity	500	1000

The Results

The results of the two break-even point methods are shown in the output to the program. From the point of view of production, introducing a new machine would reduce the break-even threshold by 24% (60% − 36%). From the point of view of immediate sales the purchase of the new machine would mean a decrease of $250 from profits. This assumes, however, that sales will not increase in proportion to increased production capacity.

The Output

```
BREAK-EVEN POINT ANALYSIS

-------------------------

BASED ON PRODUCTION CAPACITY (1)
BASED ON SALES FORECASTS (2)    ?1

TOTAL FIXED COSTS? 3000
UNIT VARIABLE COSTS? 10
UNIT SELLING PRICE? 20
MAXIMUM PRODUCTION CAPACITY? 500

BREAK-EVEN POINT = 60%
OF THE MAXIMUM PRODUCTION CAPACITY
(OR 300 UNITS)
CORRESPONDING TO SALES REVENUES
    OF $6000

CONTINUE? Y

COST-VOLUME-PROFIT ANALYSIS TABLE
----------------------------------------
UNITS    SALES    TOTAL COSTS    PROFIT
----------------------------------------
50       $1000      $3500        $-2500
100      $2000      $4000        $-2000
150      $3000      $4500        $-1500
200      $4000      $5000        $-1000
250      $5000      $5500        $-500
300      $6000      $6000        $0
350      $7000      $6500        $500
400      $8000      $7000        $1000
450      $9000      $7500        $1500
500      $10000     $8000        $2000
----------------------------------------

ANOTHER ANALYSIS? Y

BASED ON PRODUCTION CAPACITY (1)
BASED ON SALES FORECASTS (2)    ?1

TOTAL FIXED COSTS? 4500
UNIT VARIABLE COSTS? 7.5
UNIT SELLING PRICE? 20
MAXIMUM PRODUCTION CAPACITY? 1000
```

```
BREAK-EVEN POINT = 36%
OF THE MAXIMUM PRODUCTION CAPACITY
(OR 360 UNITS)
CORRESPONDING TO SALES REVENUES
    OF $7200

CONTINUE? Y

COST-VOLUME-PROFIT ANALYSIS TABLE
-----------------------------------------
UNITS    SALES    TOTAL COSTS    PROFIT
-----------------------------------------
100      $2000       $5250       $-3250
200      $4000       $6000       $-2000
300      $6000       $6750       $-750
400      $8000       $7500       $500
500     ·$10000      $8250       $1750
600      $12000      $9000       $3000
700      $14000      $9750       $4250
800      $16000      $10500      $5500
900      $18000      $11250      $6750
1000     $20000      $12000      $8000
-----------------------------------------
ANOTHER ANALYSIS? Y

BASED ON PRODUCTION CAPACITY (1)
BASED ON SALES FORECASTS (2)    ?2

TOTAL FIXED COSTS? 3000
UNIT VARIABLE COSTS? 10
UNIT SELLING PRICE? 20
EXPECTED SALES (IN UNITS)? 500

BREAK-EVEN POINT = 300 UNITS
OR $6000

TOTAL PROFIT =
   TOTAL REVENUES - TOTAL COSTS
  =    10000       -      8000

            = $2000

ANOTHER ANALYSIS? Y


BASED ON PRODUCTION CAPACITY (1)
BASED ON SALES FORECASTS (2)    ?2

TOTAL FIXED COSTS? 4500
UNIT VARIABLE COSTS? 7.5
UNIT SELLING PRICE? 20
EXPECTED SALES (IN UNITS)? 500

BREAK-EVEN POINT = 360 UNITS
OR $7200

TOTAL PROFIT =
   TOTAL REVENUES - TOTAL COSTS
  =    10000       -      8250
            = $1750

ANOTHER ANALYSIS? N
```

The Program Listing

```
1    REM        COST-VOLUME PROFIT ANALYSIS
2    REM        BUI        12/80
3    REM
4    REM        VARIABLES
5    REM        R          REVENUES
6    REM        C1         FIXED COSTS
7    REM        C2         UNIT VARIABLE COSTS
8    REM        T          TOTAL COSTS
9    REM        I          PROFIT OR INCOME
10   REM        Q          MAXIMUM PRODUCTION CAPACITY
11   REM        S          BREAK EVEN POINT
12   REM                   (% OF CAPACITY)
13   REM        E          EXPECTED SALES
20   PRINT : PRINT
30   PRINT "BREAK-EVEN POINT ANALYSIS"
40   PRINT "-------------------------"
50   PRINT : PRINT : PRINT
60   PRINT "BASED ON PRODUCTION CAPACITY (1)"
70   PRINT "BASED ON SALES FORECASTS (2)    ";
80   INPUT C
90   IF C < > 1 AND C < > 2 THEN 60
100  PRINT : PRINT
110  INPUT "TOTAL FIXED COSTS? ";C1
120  INPUT "UNIT VARIABLE COSTS? ";C2
130  INPUT "UNIT SELLING PRICE? ";P
140  IF C2 < P THEN 180
150  PRINT "*** THE SELLING PRICE MUST BE GREATER THAN"
160  PRINT "     THE UNIT VARIABLE COSTS"
170  GOTO 120
180  IF C = 2 THEN 320
190  REM  FIRST METHOD
200  INPUT "MAXIMUM PRODUCTION CAPACITY? ";Q
210  PRINT : PRINT : PRINT
220 S = C1 / ((P - C2) * Q)
230  IF S > 1 THEN  PRINT "***INPUT ERROR": GOTO 110
240  PRINT "BREAK-EVEN POINT = "; INT (10000 * S + .5) / 100;"%"
250  PRINT "OF THE MAXIMUM PRODUCTION CAPACITY"
260  PRINT "(OR "; INT (S * Q + .5);" UNITS)"
270  PRINT "CORRESPONDING TO SALES REVENUES"
280  PRINT "   OF $"; INT (100 * (S * Q * P) + .5) / 100
285  PRINT : INPUT "CONTINUE? ";Z$
290  PRINT : PRINT
300  GOTO 430
310  REM  SECOND METHOD
320  INPUT "EXPECTED SALES (IN UNITS)? ";E
330  PRINT : PRINT : PRINT
340 S = C1 / (P - C2)
350  IF S < 0 THEN  PRINT "***INPUT ERROR": GOTO 110
360  PRINT "BREAK-EVEN POINT = "; INT (100 * S + .5) / 100;" UNITS"
370  PRINT "OR $"; INT (100 * S * P + .5) / 100
380  PRINT : PRINT
390  PRINT "TOTAL PROFIT = "
395  PRINT "  TOTAL REVENUES - TOTAL COSTS"
400  PRINT "  =    ";E * P; TAB( 18);"-    ";C1 + (E * C2)
410  PRINT : PRINT  TAB( 14);"= $";E * P - (C1 + (E * C2))
420  GOTO 540
430  PRINT "COST-VOLUME-PROFIT ANALYSIS TABLE"
```

```
440  PRINT "-----------------------------------------"
450  PRINT "UNITS    SALES    TOTAL COSTS    PROFIT"
460  PRINT "-----------------------------------------"
470  FOR X =  INT (Q / 10) TO Q STEP  INT (Q / 10)
480 R = X * P
490 T = C1 + X * C2
500 I = R - T
505  DEF  FN A(X) =  INT (100 * X + .5) / 100
510  PRINT X; TAB( 8);"$"; FN A(R); TAB( 19);"$"; FN A(T); TAB( 30);"$"; FN
     A(I)
520  NEXT X
530  PRINT "-----------------------------------------"
540  PRINT : PRINT : PRINT
550  INPUT "ANOTHER ANALYSIS? ";A$
560  IF  LEFT$ (A$,1) <  > "N" THEN 50
570  END
```

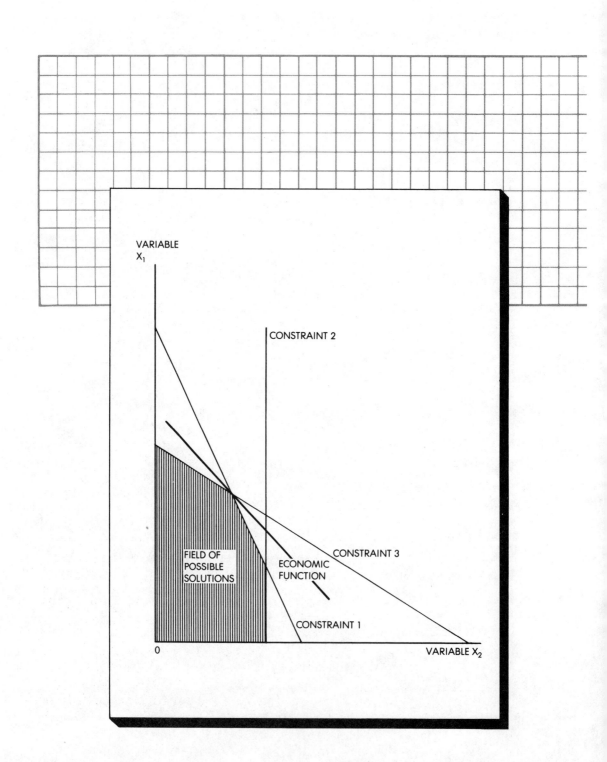

VARIABLE
X₁

CONSTRAINT 2

CONSTRAINT 3

ECONOMIC
FUNCTION

FIELD OF
POSSIBLE
SOLUTIONS

CONSTRAINT 1

0

VARIABLE X₂

CHAPTER 2
LINEAR PROGRAMMING:
THE SIMPLEX METHOD

THE METHOD

Linear programming is one of the best-known methods of linear optimization in business management. This method is also the closest mathematically to economic models of optimization, since its hypotheses are based on the scarcity of resources. In translating an economic problem into a mathematical problem, linear programming strives to *maximize results* from a given set of resources or to *minimize the resources* used for a set of desired results.

Specifically, linear programming minimizes or maximizes a linear function of several variables (called the *objective function,* or the *economic function*); this function is subject to several restrictions or constraints in the form of linear equalities or inequalities.

Several algorithms have been developed to solve linear optimization problems. Among these, the *simplex method* is by far the best known. From an operational standpoint, this general method is fast and efficient. From the economic standpoint, the method leads to statistics that are useful to management (for example, quantities of unused resources).

There are numerous applications of linear programming in business management. The method applies to all levels of activity, from production to distribution, and to all sectors of business, from agriculture to aviation.

THE PROGRAM

The BASIC program presented in this chapter implements the simplex method; this method uses an iterative process that identifies an initial feasible solution, then searches to see if there is a better solution. When the best solution is found, the process resumes. The advantage of this program over other versions of the simplex method is that the process of inputting values is clear and simple. The user can input the raw data from the linear model without having to rearrange them first. The program itself identifies and defines the variables to be input, including specific variables related to the simplex method.

The user of this program follows five simple steps for input:

1. define the type of economic function (maximization or minimization)
2. identify the decision variables (production volume, budget, etc.)
3. construct the objective function in linear form
4. determine the constraints expressed in linear form
5. classify the constraints in the following order:
   — less than or equal to ($<=$)
   — greater than or equal to ($>=$)
   — equality ($=$)

The simplex algorithm performs its iterative process on a *basis* (matrix) called the simplex tableau. This tableau is simply a matrix transformation of the linear programming model from *canonical* form to a *standard* form. This transformation is effected by the introduction of *slack variables* and *artificial variables.* Lines 100 to 850 construct this tableau in the simplest way possible; the user inputs the data in canonical form, and the program carries on from there. Lines 210 to 550 identify and print the specific variables of the simplex method (decision variables, slack variables, and artificial variables).

Lines 870 to 1270 prepare and print the simplex tableau. Optimization analysis is performed in lines 1290 to 1570. When an optimal solution is identified, lines 1590 to 1700 print the solution and the results of the problem. If the test shows that optimization has not been attained, however, another transformation of the simplex tableau is necessary: first a new *basic variable* is determined (lines 1300 to 1340), a variable is taken from the basis (lines 1740 to 1800), and then the data of the tableau are transformed (lines 1840 to 1990).

APPLICATION EXAMPLE

The Problem

Viva, Inc., is a beverage producer, founded in 1931. The company produces beer, lemon soda, and mineral water. Traditionally, the company has enjoyed a stable and loyal clientele. However, Viva has recently experienced a sharp rise in production costs. An appraisal of the production line has revealed that aging and obsolete equipment is responsible for the rise in costs.

Viva has decided to liquidate its present equipment, which is already fully depreciated, and to install an entirely new production system. The new system will be divided into two distinct parts—one for beer and the other for lemon soda and mineral water.

Viva must now decide how to partition the production capacity among the three products in a way that will maximize profits. The production, accounting, and marketing departments all have requirements that must be taken into account when this decision is made.

The Data

1. Specification of the type of economic factor: Maximize profit.

2. Identification of the decision variables:

   x_1 = quantity of beer (units of 1000 liters)
   x_2 = quantity of lemon soda (units of 1000 liters)
   x_3 = quantity of mineral water (units of 1000 liters)

3. Formulation of the linear economic function: The accounting department has supplied the following figures for the contribution margins (per 1000 liters) of each product:

beer	$250
lemon soda	$190
mineral water	$175

   The economic relationship between the three decision variables can thus be expressed as:

   Profit (to be maximized) = $250x_1 + 190x_2 + 175x_3$

4. Determination and classification of constraints: According to the production manager and his technical personnel, the maximum capacity of the new production machinery is:

Beer production line

    Beer   7000 liters per day

Lemon Soda/Mineral Water production line
If devoted exclusively to:

    Lemon Soda   53,300 liters per day
    Mineral Water   80,000 liters per day

In other words, in the second production line, lemon soda takes 50% longer to produce than mineral water.

The company has 70 man-hours of labor available per day. The technical experts claim that 2 man-hours are required to produce 1000 liters of beer, 1 man-hour for 1000 liters of lemon soda, and .5 man-hour for 1000 liters of mineral water.

In addition to these production constraints, the marketing department requires that at least 20,000 liters of lemon soda be produced per day to meet the demand for that product.

The data from this problem are summarized in the table below:

Product	Decision Variable	Production		Labor	Contribution Margin	Marketing Requirement
		System 1	System 2			
Beer	x_1	1	0	2	250	0
Soda	x_2	0	1.5	1	190	20
Mineral Water	x_3	0	1	0.5	175	0
Maximum capacity		7	80	70		

In the linear programming method, the problem is presented as follows:

$$\text{Maximize:} \quad 250x_1 + 190x_2 + 175x_3$$
$$\text{Constraints:} \quad x_1 \qquad\qquad\qquad \leq 7$$
$$1.5x_2 + \quad x_3 \leq 80$$
$$2x_1 + \quad x_2 + \quad .5x_3 \leq 70$$
$$x_2 \qquad\qquad \geq 20$$

The Results

Study the output from the program. Unless production or market conditions change, Viva's optimal production level can be summarized as follows:

Beer	7,000 liters per day
Lemon Soda	20,000 liters per day
Mineral Water	50,000 liters per day

This production schedule results in a labor surplus of 11 man-hours, and in a daily profit of $14,300.

---**The Output**---

```
LINEAR PROGRAMMING
------------------


ECONOMIC FUNCTION:
MAXIMIZE OR MINIMIZE (MAX/MIN)? MAX
NUMBER OF DECISION VARIABLES? 3


NUMBER OF CONSTRAINTS
(EXCLUDING NONNEGATIVITY CONSTRAINTS):
LESS THAN OR EQUAL TO?     3
GREATER THAN OR EQUAL TO? 1
EQUAL?                     0


DEFINITION OF VARIABLE INDICES:

DECISION VARIABLE 1 = X(1)
DECISION VARIABLE 2 = X(2)
DECISION VARIABLE 3 = X(3)

SLACK VARIABLE(S) OF
LESS-THAN-OR-EQUAL-TO CONSTRAINTS:
CONSTRAINT 1 = X(4)
CONSTRAINT 2 = X(5)
CONSTRAINT 3 = X(6)

SLACK VARIABLE(S) OF
GREATER-THAN-OR-EQUAL-TO CONSTRAINTS
(SURPLUS VARIABLES):
CONSTRAINT 4 = X(8)

ARTIFICIAL VARIABLE(S) FOR THE
GREATER-THAN-OR-EQUAL-TO AND
EQUALITY CONSTRAINTS:
CONSTRAINT 4 = X(7)
```

```
COEFFICIENTS OF THE OBJECTIVE FUNCTION:
COEF. OF DECISION VARIABLE 1 ?250
COEF. OF DECISION VARIABLE 2 ?190
COEF. OF DECISION VARIABLE 3 ?175

VALUE OF THE RIGHT SIDE
  OF CONSTRAINT 1      ?7
VALUE OF THE RIGHT SIDE
  OF CONSTRAINT 2      ?80
VALUE OF THE RIGHT SIDE
  OF CONSTRAINT 3      ?70
VALUE OF THE RIGHT SIDE
  OF CONSTRAINT 4      ?20

CONSTRAINT COEFFICIENTS:
COEFFICIENT OF CONSTRAINT #1
--DECISION VARIABLE 1 ?1
--DECISION VARIABLE 2 ?0
--DECISION VARIABLE 3 ?0
COEFFICIENT OF CONSTRAINT #2
--DECISION VARIABLE 1 ?0
--DECISION VARIABLE 2 ?1.5
--DECISION VARIABLE 3 ?1
COEFFICIENT OF CONSTRAINT #3
--DECISION VARIABLE 1 ?2
--DECISION VARIABLE 2 ?1
--DECISION VARIABLE 3 ?.5
COEFFICIENT OF CONSTRAINT #4
--DECISION VARIABLE 1 ?0
--DECISION VARIABLE 2 ?1
--DECISION VARIABLE 3 ?0


ITERATION #0
------------
BASIC VARIABLES       VALUE
      X(4)              7
      X(5)              80
      X(6)              70
      X(7)              20

VARIABLES OF THE SIMPLEX TABLEAU
X(4),X(5),X(6),X(7),X(1),X(2),X(3),X(8),

MATRIX OF COEFFICIENTS A(I,J):
1    0    0    0    1    0     0     0
0    1    0    0    0    1.5   1     0
0    0    1    0    2    1     .5    0
0    0    0    1    0    1     0    -1

MARGINAL PROFIT COEFFICIENTS Z(J)-C(J):
0    0    0    0    250   10190   175   -10000

ECONOMIC FUNCTION Z = 200000


CONTINUE? Y
```

```
ITERATION #1
------------
BASIC VARIABLES          VALUE
     X(4)                 7
     X(5)                50
     X(6)                50
     X(2)                20

VARIABLES OF THE SIMPLEX TABLEAU
X(4),X(5),X(6),X(7),X(1),X(2),X(3),X(8),

MATRIX OF COEFFICIENTS A(I,J):
1    0    0    0    1    0    0    0
0    1    0   -1.5  0    0    1    1.5
0    0    1   -1    2    0    .5   1
0    0    0    1    0    1    0   -1

MARGINAL PROFIT COEFFICIENTS Z(J)-C(J):
0    0    0   -10190  250   0    175  190

ECONOMIC FUNCTION Z = -3800


CONTINUE? Y


ITERATION #2
------------
BASIC VARIABLES          VALUE
     X(1)                 7
     X(5)                50
     X(6)                36
     X(2)                20

VARIABLES OF THE SIMPLEX TABLEAU
X(4),X(5),X(6),X(7),X(1),X(2),X(3),X(8),

MATRIX OF COEFFICIENTS A(I,J):
1    0    0    0    1    0    0    0
0    1    0   -1.5  0    0    1    1.5
-2   0    1   -1    0    0    .5   1
0    0    0    1    0    1    0   -1

MARGINAL PROFIT COEFFICIENTS Z(J)-C(J):
-250   0    0   -10190  0    0    175  190

ECONOMIC FUNCTION Z = -5550


CONTINUE? Y


ITERATION #3
------------
BASIC VARIABLES          VALUE
     X(1)                 7
     X(8)                33.3333333
     X(6)                 2.66666667
     X(2)                53.3333333
```

```
VARIABLES OF THE SIMPLEX TABLEAU
X(4),X(5),X(6),X(7),X(1),X(2),X(3),X(8),

MATRIX OF COEFFICIENTS A(I,J):
1     0     0     0     1     0     0     0
0     .67   0    -1     0     0     .67   1
-2    -.67  1     0     0     0    -.17   0
0     .67   0     0     0     1     .67   0

MARGINAL PROFIT COEFFICIENTS Z(J)-C(J):
-250   -126.67   0   -10000   0   0   48.33   0

ECONOMIC FUNCTION Z = -11883.3333


CONTINUE? Y


ITERATION #4
------------
BASIC VARIABLES          VALUE
      X(1)                 7
      X(3)                50
      X(6)                11
      X(2)                20

VARIABLES OF THE SIMPLEX TABLEAU
X(4),X(5),X(6),X(7),X(1),X(2),X(3),X(8),

MATRIX OF COEFFICIENTS A(I,J):
1     0     0     0     1     0     0     0
0     1     0    -1.5   0     0     1     1.5
-2    -.5   1    -.25   0     0     0     .25
0     0     0     1     0     1     0    -1

MARGINAL PROFIT COEFFICIENTS Z(J)-C(J):
-250   -175   0   -9927.5   0   0   0   -72.5

ECONOMIC FUNCTION Z = -14300


CONTINUE? Y

 *** OPTIMAL SOLUTION FOUND ***
 *** AFTER 5 ITERATIONS      ***

---------------------------------------
 DECISION VARIABLE     VALUE
---------------------------------------
      X(1)      =         7
      X(3)      =        50
      X(6)      =        11
      X(2)      =        20
NOTE:
ALL VARIABLES NOT SHOWN
IN THIS TABLE HAVE VALUES OF ZERO.

---------------------------------------
      MAXIMUM     Z = 14300
---------------------------------------
```

┌─ **The Program Listing** ─────────────────────────────────────

```
1    REM        LINEAR OPTIMIZATION BY THE SIMPLEX METHOD
2    REM        BUI      4/81
3    REM
4    REM        VARIABLES
5    REM        M         TOTAL NUMBER OF CONSTRAINTS
6    REM        MN        NUMBER OF DECISION VARIABLES
7    REM        N         TOTAL NUMBER OF VARIABLES
8    REM        NB        NUMBER OF >= CONSTRAINTS
9    REM        NE        NUMBER OF = CONSTRAINTS
10   REM        NS        NUMBER OF <= CONSTRAINTS
11   REM        OB        ECONOMIC FUNCTION
12   REM        XJ(I)     VECTOR IDENTIFYING  THE VARIABLES
13   REM        ZC(I)     COEFFICIENTS OF MARGINAL PROFITS
14   REM        A(I,J)    MATRIX OF TECHNOLOGICAL COEFFICIENTS
15   REM        B(I)      VECTOR OF VALUES OF THE RIGHT-HAND
16   REM                  SIDE OF THE CONSTRAINTS
17   REM        CJ(I)     COEFFICIENTS OF THE OBJECTIVE FUNCTION
18   REM
30   PRINT "LINEAR PROGRAMMING"
40   PRINT "------------------": PRINT : PRINT : PRINT
50   PRINT "ECONOMIC FUNCTION: "
60   INPUT "MAXIMIZE OR MINIMIZE (MAX/MIN)? ";C$
70   IF  LEFT$ (C$,2) <  > "MA" AND  LEFT$ (C$,2) <  > "MI" THEN 60
80   IF  LEFT$ (C$,2) = "MI" THEN PT =  - 1: GOTO 100
90   PT = 1
100  INPUT "NUMBER OF DECISION VARIABLES? ";MN
110  PRINT : PRINT
120  PRINT "NUMBER OF CONSTRAINTS"
130  PRINT "(EXCLUDING NONNEGATIVITY CONSTRAINTS):"
140  INPUT "LESS THAN OR EQUAL TO?      ";NS
150  INPUT "GREATER THAN OR EQUAL TO? ";NB
160  INPUT "EQUAL?                    ";NE
170  M = NS + NB + NE: REM    M = TOTAL CONSTRAINTS
180  N = M + MN + NB: REM   N = TOTAL VARIABLES
190  DIM B(M),CI(N),CJ(N),Z(N),ZC(N),XI(N),XJ(N),A(M,N)
200  REM
210  REM        IDENTIFICATION OF DECISION VARIABLES,
220  REM        SLACK VARIABLES, AND ARTIFICIAL VARIABLES
230  PRINT : PRINT
240  PRINT "DEFINITION OF VARIABLE INDICES:": PRINT
250  K = 1: FOR J = M + 1 TO M + MN
260  PRINT "DECISION VARIABLE ";K;
270  XJ(J) = K
280  PRINT " = X(";XJ(J);")"
290  K = K + 1: NEXT J: PRINT
300  IF NS <  = 0 THEN 390
310  PRINT "SLACK VARIABLE(S) OF "
320  PRINT "LESS-THAN-OR-EQUAL-TO CONSTRAINTS:"
330  K = MN + 1: FOR J = 1 TO NS
340  PRINT "CONSTRAINT ";J;
350  XJ(J) = K
360  PRINT " = X(";XJ(J);")"
370  K = K + 1: NEXT J: PRINT
380  FOR I = 1 TO N:CJ(I) = 0: NEXT I
390  IF NB = 0 THEN 470
400  PRINT "SLACK VARIABLE(S) OF"
```

```
410   PRINT "GREATER-THAN-OR-EQUAL-TO CONSTRAINTS"
415   PRINT "(SURPLUS VARIABLES):"
420  K = M + MN + 1: FOR J = M + MN + 1 TO N
430   PRINT "CONSTRAINT ";J + NS - M - MN;
440  XJ(J) = K
450   PRINT " = X(";XJ(J);")"
460  K = K + 1: NEXT J: PRINT
470   IF NB = 0 AND NE = 0 THEN 560
480   PRINT "ARTIFICIAL VARIABLE(S) FOR THE"
490   PRINT "GREATER-THAN-OR-EQUAL-TO AND"
495   PRINT "EQUALITY CONSTRAINTS:"
500  K = MN + NS + 1: FOR J = NS + 1 TO M
510   PRINT "CONSTRAINT ";J;
520  XJ(J) = K
530   PRINT " = X(";XJ(J);")"
540  CJ(J) = 10000
550  K = K + 1: NEXT J: PRINT
560   FOR I = 1 TO M:XI(I) = XJ(I): NEXT I
570   PRINT "COEFFICIENTS OF THE OBJECTIVE FUNCTION: "
580   FOR I = M + 1 TO M + MN
590   PRINT "COEF. OF DECISION VARIABLE ";I - M;" ";
600   INPUT CJ(I)
610  CJ(I) = CJ(I) * PT * ( - 1)
620   NEXT I: PRINT
630   FOR I = 1 TO M
640   PRINT "VALUE OF THE RIGHT SIDE"
645   PRINT "  OF CONSTRAINT ";I;"        ";
650   INPUT B(I): NEXT I
660   REM       CONSTRUCT THE UNIT MATRIX
670   FOR I = 1 TO M: FOR J = 1 TO N
680   IF I < > J THEN 710
690  A(I,J) = 1
700   GOTO 720
710  A(I,J) = 0
720   NEXT J,I
730   PRINT
740   PRINT "CONSTRAINT COEFFICIENTS:"
750   FOR I = 1 TO M
760   PRINT "COEFFICIENT OF CONSTRAINT #";I
770   FOR J = M + 1 TO M + MN
780   PRINT "--DECISION VARIABLE ";J - M;" ";
790   INPUT A(I,J)
800   NEXT J,I
810   IF NB = 0 THEN 870
820   REM        INTRODUCE THE COEFFICIENTS OF THE SURPLUS VARIABLES
830   FOR I = 1 TO NB
840  A(NS + 1,M + MN + I) =  - 1
850   NEXT I
860   REM       SIMPLEX ALGORITHM
870   FOR I = 1 TO M: FOR J = 1 TO N
880   IF XI(I) < > XJ(J) THEN 900
890  CI(I) = CJ(J)
900   NEXT J,I
910  IT = 0
920   FOR J = 1 TO N
930  Z(J) = 0
940   FOR I = 1 TO M
950  Z(J) = Z(J) + CI(I) * A(I,J)
```

```
960   NEXT I
970 ZC(J) = Z(J) - CJ(J)
980   NEXT J
990 OB = 0
1000  FOR I = 1 TO M
1010 OB = OB + CI(I) * B(I)
1020  NEXT I
1030  PRINT : PRINT
1040  PRINT "ITERATION #";IT
1050  PRINT "------------"
1060  PRINT "BASIC VARIABLES        VALUE"
1070  FOR I = 1 TO M
1080  PRINT  TAB( 6);"X(";XI(I);")"; TAB( 26);B(I): NEXT I
1090  PRINT :N1 = 1:N2 = 8
1100  IF N2 < = N THEN 1120
1110 N2 = N
1120  PRINT "VARIABLES OF THE SIMPLEX TABLEAU"
1130  FOR I = N1 TO N2
1140  PRINT "X(";XJ(I);"),";
1145  NEXT I
1150  PRINT : PRINT
1160  PRINT "MATRIX OF COEFFICIENTS A(I,J):"
1170  FOR I = 1 TO M:K = 0: FOR J = N1 TO N2
1180  PRINT  TAB( 5 * K + 1); INT (100 * A(I,J) + .5) / 100;:K = K + 1
1190  NEXT J: PRINT : NEXT I: PRINT
1200  PRINT "MARGINAL PROFIT COEFFICIENTS Z(J)-C(J):"
1210  FOR I = N1 TO N2
1220  PRINT  INT (100 * ZC(I) + .5) / 100;"   ";
1230  NEXT I: PRINT
1240  IF N2 > = N THEN 1270
1250 N1 = N1 + 8:N2 = N2 + 8
1260  GOTO 1100
1270  PRINT : PRINT "ECONOMIC FUNCTION Z = ";OB: PRINT
1280  PRINT : INPUT "CONTINUE? ";C$
1290 IT = IT + 1:CM = ZC(1):JM = 1
1300  FOR J = 2 TO N
1310  IF ZC(J) < CM THEN 1330
1320 CM = ZC(J):JM = J
1330  NEXT J
1340  IF CM > 0 THEN 1740
1350 M3 = M + MN:MO = M + 1
1360  IF M = NS THEN 1420
1370  FOR I = 1 TO M
1380 M4 = NS + 1
1390  FOR J = M4 TO M
1400  IF XI(I) = XJ(J) THEN 1720
1410  NEXT J,I
1420  FOR K = MO TO M3
1430  FOR I = 1 TO M
1440  IF XJ(K) = XI(I) GOTO 1470
1450  NEXT I
1460  IF ZC(K) = 0 THEN 1490
1470  NEXT K
1480  GOTO 1500
1490  PRINT " *** SEVERAL OPTIMAL SOLUTIONS POSSIBLE ***"
1500  PRINT : PRINT : PRINT
1510  PRINT " *** OPTIMAL SOLUTION FOUND ***"
1520  PRINT " *** AFTER ";IT;" ITERATIONS      ***"
```

```
1530   FOR I = 1 TO M
1540   IF B(I) < > 0 THEN 1570
1550   PRINT : PRINT " *** DEGENERATE SOLUTION *** "
1560   GOTO 1580
1570   NEXT I
1580   PRINT
1590   PRINT "-----------------------------------"
1600   PRINT "  DECISION VARIABLE    VALUE"
1610   PRINT "-----------------------------------"
1620   FOR I = 1 TO M
1630   PRINT  TAB( 8);"X(";XI(I);")"; TAB( 16);"="; TAB( 25);B(I)
1640   NEXT I
1650   PRINT "NOTE: ": PRINT "ALL VARIABLES NOT SHOWN "
1660   PRINT "IN THIS TABLE HAVE VALUES OF ZERO."
1670   PRINT "-----------------------------------"
1680   IF PT = 1 THEN  PRINT  TAB( 5);"MAXIMUM   Z = "; ABS (OB)
1690   IF PT = - 1 THEN  PRINT  TAB( 5);"MINIMUM   Z = "; ABS (OB)
1700   PRINT "-----------------------------------"
1710   STOP
1720   PRINT : PRINT " *** UNBOUNDED SOLUTION ***"
1730   STOP
1740 XM = 1.0E25:IM = 0
1750   FOR I = 1 TO M
1760   IF A(I,JM) < = 0 THEN 1800
1770   XX = B(I) / A(I,JM)
1780   IF XX > = XM THEN 1800
1790 XM = XX:IM = I
1800   NEXT I
1810   IF IM > 0 THEN 1840
1820   PRINT " *** SOLUTION IMPOSSIBLE ***"
1830   STOP
1840 XX = A(IM,JM)
1850 B(IM) = B(IM) / XX
1860   FOR J = 1 TO N
1870 A(IM,J) = A(IM,J) / XX
1880   NEXT J
1890   FOR I = 1 TO M
1900   IF I = IM THEN 1960
1910 XX = A(I,JM)
1920 B(I) = B(I) - XX * B(IM)
1930   FOR J = 1 TO N
1940 A(I,J) = A(I,J) - XX * A(IM,J)
1950   NEXT J
1960   NEXT I
1970 CI(IM) = CJ(JM)
1980 XI(IM) = XJ(JM)
1990   GOTO 920
```

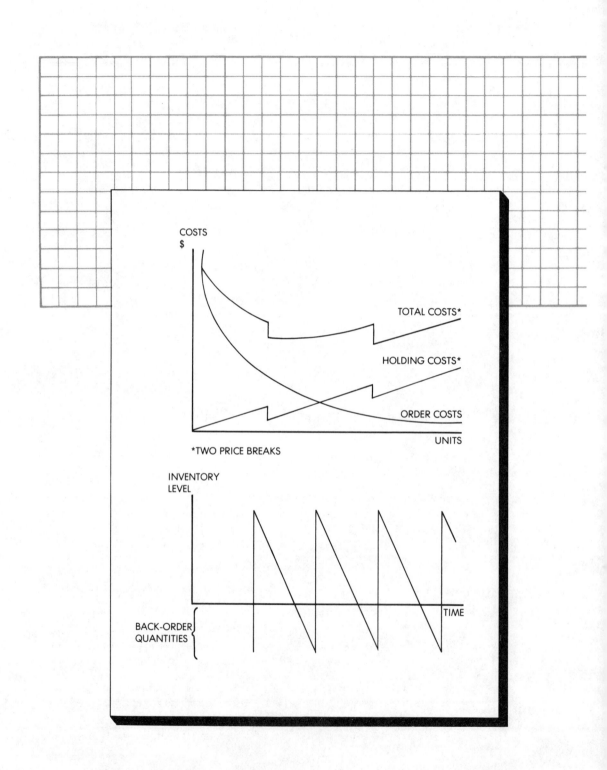

COSTS
$

TOTAL COSTS*

HOLDING COSTS*

ORDER COSTS

UNITS

*TWO PRICE BREAKS

INVENTORY
LEVEL

TIME

BACK-ORDER
QUANTITIES

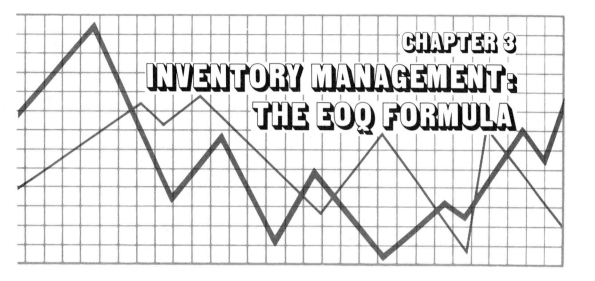

CHAPTER 3
INVENTORY MANAGEMENT:
THE EOQ FORMULA

THE METHOD

Inventory management occupies an important place among general business management tasks. Its decisive role can be explained by at least three facts:

- First, a business must maintain a minimum inventory, keeping an equilibrium between incoming and outgoing products.

- Second, a precautionary inventory must be maintained for unexpected demands.

- Finally, since business is dependent on the overall economic climate, it is important to have adequate inventory reserves to meet the needs of future expansion during the time of an economic upswing.

The different, and sometimes conflicting, interests within a business can further complicate the total picture. The production manager needs to maintain a steady production rate to stabilize employment and to achieve a high level of productivity. The commercial department wants above all to guarantee the best possible service to clients in order to attain sales objectives, or better yet, to beat the competition. The accounting department wants to maintain a low-level inventory to free up funds for meeting operating costs. In short, too small an inventory can slow down production and cause loss of sales, while too large an inventory leads to unnecessary inventory costs.

The model outlined in this chapter, known as the *Economic-Order-Quantity* (EOQ) formula, comes from operations research; it leads to at least a partial solution to this dilemma. The objective of the model is to determine the optimal inventory to order corresponding to the lowest cost. The model is based on the fact that some inventory costs (such as storage costs, product deterioration, loss, theft, and so on) *increase* when the average inventory volume is higher, whereas other costs (such as ordering costs, opportunity losses due to shortages, etc.) *decrease* when a higher level of inventory is maintained.

THE PROGRAM

The EOQ program determines the optimal inventory reorder quantity with the least corresponding cost (including ordering costs, storage costs, and losses due to shortages). The program also takes into account the value of any discounts that may be accorded to large orders; this version allows input of two levels of unit-cost discounting.

In addition, limitations of storage space and cash on hand available for inventory purchases are two constraints that the EOQ program figures into its calculation of the optimal ordering policy. (Actually, these two limitations are combined in one category—maximum inventory capacity.)

The basic formula of the EOQ model is relatively simple:

$$Q = \sqrt{\frac{2D \cdot C}{P \cdot I}}$$

where:

Q = EOQ

D = annual demand in units

P = unit purchase price

C = cost per order

I = inventory cost

However, when we wish to include certain, more realistic, factors—such as price discounts, shortages, and limited inventory capacity—the formula becomes more complex. The program presented in this chapter includes formulas to account for all of these factors.

The input section is in lines 60 to 320. As usual, it is in conversational form and contains error-checking. Lines 345 to 590 organize the input data for the appropriate situation: no discount, one discount, two discounts, and limited inventory capacity.

Lines 830 to 960 compute the EOQ and the total inventory costs for different elements of the arrays Q and P, using the formula above. For shortages, the corresponding cost is calculated for the period in which the inventory level does not meet the demand (lines 620 to 810).

Lines 980 to 1090 find the order quantity corresponding to the minimum total costs when price discounts are used. Lines 1130 to 1290 deal with limited inventory capacity. When the calculated EOQ is less than the maximum capacity, the ordering policy is not affected. Otherwise it is necessary to compute the ordering quantity that minimizes total costs while not exceeding the maximum inventory capacity.

Finally, two subroutines print the results. The second subroutine (at line 3000) is used to describe the problem of limited inventory capacity.

APPLICATION EXAMPLE

The Problem

Soundpath, Inc., is a company that specializes in the production of soundproofing materials. To package its products it receives a standing monthly order of 125 specially made cartons from one of its suppliers. The basic price of one carton is $2; however, Soundpath has recently received a new price schedule from the supplier, offering the following price reductions for quantity orders:

Number of Cartons	Unit Price
0–199	$2.00
200–399	1.75
400 and over	1.50

Soundpath intends to take advantage of this offer by replanning its inventory ordering policy.

The Data

The accounting department has supplied the following data:

Number of cartons used per year	1500 units
Cost of one order (administrative costs, delivery, etc.)	$10
Unit holding costs (storage, obsolescence, insurance, etc.)	10% of the price of the product
Shortage costs (backorder costs, customer dissatisfaction, etc.)	.50 per unit
Maximum inventory capacity	180 units

The Results

1. Present total inventory costs:

    total cost = cost of units ordered
                + ordering costs
                + inventory storage costs
                = 1500 units × $2.
                + 12 orders × $10.
                + 1500/2 × $.20
                = $3270.

2. Total inventory costs as calculated by EOQ:

    total cost = $2638.
    (See output from program.)

Decision

The new inventory management policy calls for an order of 200 units approximately every seven weeks. This policy takes advantage of the supplier's quantity-order price-reduction schedule to the extent possible, given Soundpath's limited inventory storage capacity.

```
┌─The Output ─────────────────────────────────────
│
│   OPTIMAL INVENTORY MANAGEMENT
│   ----------------------------
│
│
│   ANNUAL DEMAND FOR ITEM (IN UNITS)? 1500
│
│   PRICE:
│   NO REDUCTION     <0>
│   ONE REDUCTION    <1>
│   TWO REDUCTIONS <2> ?2
│
```

```
UNIT PRICE OF PRODUCT? 2

UNIT PRICE WITH FIRST REDUCTION? 1.75

QUANTITY REQUIRED FOR
FIRST REDUCTION?     200

UNIT PRICE WITH SECOND REDUCTION? 1.50

QUANTITY REQUIRED FOR
SECOND REDUCTION?    400

COST OF ONE ORDER? 10

UNIT HOLDING COSTS
(PERCENT OF PURCHASE PRICE) ? 10

SHORTAGE COSTS? .50

LIMITED INVENTORY CAPACITY
YES <1>, NO <0>   ?1

MAXIMUM CAPACITY OF INVENTORY? 180



RESULTS OF THE EOQ MODEL:
----------------------------------------

OPTIMAL ORDER QUANTITY = 400 UNITS.
OPTIMAL INVENTORY      = 308 UNITS.
UNIT PURCHASE PRICE    = $1.5.
TOTAL HOLDING COSTS    = $2273.12.
----------------------------------------

ORDERS SHOULD BE PLACED 3.8
TIMES PER YEAR.
----------------------------------------



CONTINUE? Y


INVENTORY CAPACITY IS LESS THAN OPTIMAL
----------------------------------------

WITH LIMITED INVENTORY CAPACITY...
RESULTS OF THE EOQ MODEL:
----------------------------------------

OPTIMAL ORDER QUANTITY = 200 UNITS.
OPTIMAL INVENTORY      = 148 UNITS.
UNIT PURCHASE PRICE    = $1.75.
TOTAL HOLDING COSTS    = $2638.15.
----------------------------------------

ORDERS SHOULD BE PLACED 7.5
TIMES PER YEAR.
----------------------------------------


COSTS DUE TO LIMITED CAPACITY = $365.03
----------------------------------------
```

---The Program Listing---

```
1    REM       ECONOMIC ORDER QUANTITY (EOQ)
2    REM       BUI            10/81
3    REM
4    REM       VARIABLES
5    REM       CC        COST OF ONE ORDER
6    REM       CM        MAXIMUM INVENTORY CAPACITY
7    REM       CR        SHORTAGE COSTS
8    REM       CT(I)     TOTAL COSTS AT INVENTORY
9    REM                 LEVELS Q(I) AND Q1(I)
10   REM       D         ANNUAL DEMAND
11   REM       DS        UNIT HOLDING COSTS
12   REM       P(I)      UNIT PRICE ARRAY:
13   REM          P(1)   BASIC PRICE
14   REM          P(2)   PRICE WITH FIRST REDUCTION, AT LEVEL R1
15   REM          P(3)   PRICE WITH FIRST REDUCTION, BEYOND LEVEL R1
16   REM          P(4)   PRICE WITH SECOND REDUCTION, AT LEVEL R2
17   REM          P(5)   PRICE WITH SECOND REDUCTION, BEYOND LEVEL R2
18   REM          P(6)   PRICE AT LEVEL CM
19   REM       R1        QUANTITY REQUIRED FOR FIRST DISCOUNT
20   REM       R2        QUANTITY REQUIRED FOR SECOND DISCOUNT
21   REM       Q(I)      ARRAY OF ORDER QUANTITIES CORRESPONDING TO P(I)
22   REM       Q1(I)     MOST ECONOMIC INVENTORY LEVEL FOR Q(I)
23   REM
24   PRINT : PRINT : PRINT
25   REM       ROUNDING FUNCTIONS
27   DEF  FN A(X) =  INT (100 * X + .5) / 100
28   DEF  FN B(X) =  INT (X + .5)
29   DEF  FN C(X) =  INT (10 * X + .5) / 10
30   PRINT "OPTIMAL INVENTORY MANAGEMENT"
40   PRINT "-------------------------"
50   PRINT : PRINT : PRINT
60   REM       DATA INPUT
70   DIM P(6),Q(6),Q1(6),CT(6)
80   INPUT "ANNUAL DEMAND FOR ITEM (IN UNITS)? ";D
90   PRINT :XL = 1.E20
100  PRINT "PRICE:"
110  PRINT "NO REDUCTION    <0>"
120  PRINT "ONE REDUCTION   <1>"
130  INPUT "TWO REDUCTIONS <2> ?";X1
140  IF X1 < 0 OR X1 > 2 THEN 100
150  PRINT
160  INPUT "UNIT PRICE OF PRODUCT? ";P(1): PRINT
170  IF X1 = 0 THEN 235
180  INPUT "UNIT PRICE WITH FIRST REDUCTION? ";P(3): PRINT
185  IF P(3) > = P(1) THEN 160
190  PRINT "QUANTITY REQUIRED FOR"
195  INPUT "FIRST REDUCTION?      ";R1
200  PRINT
210  IF X1 < > 2 THEN 240
220  INPUT "UNIT PRICE WITH SECOND REDUCTION? ";P(5): PRINT
225  IF P(5) > = P(3) THEN 180
230  PRINT "QUANTITY REQUIRED FOR"
233  INPUT "SECOND REDUCTION?      ";R2
235  IF R2 < = R1 THEN 190
237  PRINT
240  INPUT "COST OF ONE ORDER? ";CC
250  PRINT
260  PRINT "UNIT HOLDING COSTS"
```

```
265   INPUT "(PERCENT OF PURCHASE PRICE) ? ";DS
270  DS = DS / 100: PRINT
280   INPUT "SHORTAGE COSTS? ";CR
290   PRINT
300   PRINT "LIMITED INVENTORY CAPACITY"
305   INPUT "YES <1>, NO <0>  ?";X2: PRINT
310   IF X2 = 0 THEN CM = XL: GOTO 330
320   INPUT "MAXIMUM CAPACITY OF INVENTORY? ";CM
330  R3 = CM
340   PRINT : PRINT : PRINT
345   REM         IDENTIFICATION OF VARIABLES
350   REM         NO DISCOUNT
360   IF X1 <  > 0 THEN 395
370  R1 = XL
380  P(3) = P(1)
385   GOTO 400
390   REM         ONE DISCOUNT
395   IF X1 <  > 1 THEN 450
400  R2 = XL
410  P(5) = P(3)
430   REM         TWO DISCOUNTS
450  P(2) = P(3)
460  P(4) = P(5)
470   REM         INVENTORY LIMITATIONS
500   IF CM = R1 THEN P(6) = P(2): GOTO 590
510   IF CM < R1 THEN P(6) = P(1): GOTO 590
520   IF CM = R2 THEN P(6) = P(4): GOTO 590
530   IF CM < R2 THEN P(6) = P(3): GOTO 590
540  P(6) = P(5)
590  Q(2) = R1:Q(4) = R2:Q(6) = R3
600   IF CR = 0 THEN 830
610   REM         SHORTAGES
620  Q1(6) = Q(6)
630   FOR I = 1 TO 5 STEP 2
640  Q1(I) =  SQR (2 * D * CC * CR / (P(I) * DS * (DS * P(I) + CR)))
650  Q(I) =  SQR ((2 * CC * D * (DS * P(I) + CR)) / (DS * P(I) * CR))
660   NEXT I
670   FOR I = 2 TO 4 STEP 2
680   IF Q(I) <  > XL THEN 710
690  Q1(I) = XL
700   GOTO 720
710  Q1(I) = (Q(I) * CR) / (P(I) * DS + CR)
720   NEXT I
730   IF Q1(6) = XL THEN 750
740  Q(6) =  SQR ((2 * CC * D + Q1(6) ^ 2 * (CR + P(6) * DS)) / CR)
750   FOR I = 1 TO 6
760   IF Q(I) = XL THEN 800
770  S1 = (CC * D / Q(I) + DS * P(I) * Q1(I) ^ 2) / (2 * Q(I))
780  CT(I) = S1 + (D * P(I)) + ((CR * (Q(I) - Q1(I)) ^ 2) / (2 * Q(I)))
790   GOTO 810
800  CT(I) = XL
810   NEXT I
820   GOTO 980
830   REM         NO SHORTAGES
840   FOR I = 1 TO 5 STEP 2
850  Q(I) =  SQR ((2 * CC * D) / (DS * P(I)))
860   NEXT I
```

```
870   REM       EXAMINE COSTS WITH DISCOUNTS
880   FOR I = 1 TO 6
890   IF Q(I) = XL THEN 920
900 CT(I) = (CC * D / Q(I) + P(I) * D + P(I) * DS * Q(I) / 2)
910   GOTO 930
920 CT(I) = XL
930   NEXT I
940   FOR I = 1 TO 6
950 Q1(I) = Q(I)
960   NEXT I
970   REM       TEST
980   IF Q(1) > Q(2) THEN CT(1) = XL
990   IF Q(2) > Q(3) THEN 1010
1000  IF Q(3) < = Q(4) THEN 1020
1010 CT(3) = XL
1020  IF Q(4) < = Q(5) THEN 1050
1030  REM       EOQ WITH UNLIMITED CAPACITY (CM = XL)
1040 CT(5) = XL
1050 M = 1:Q0 = Q(1):S0 = Q1(1):CT = CT(1)
1060  FOR I = 1 TO 5
1070  IF CT < = CT(I) THEN 1090
1080 M = I:Q0 = Q(I):S0 = Q1(I):CT = CT(I)
1090  NEXT I
1100 T8 = CT: REM       CALCULATE COSTS OF LIMITED INVENTORY CAPACITY
1110  GOSUB 2500: REM       OUTPUT WITH CM = XL
1115  INPUT "CONTINUE? ";A$: PRINT
1120  REM       TEST WITH LIMITED CAPACITY
1130  IF CM = XL THEN 9999: REM       END
1140  FOR I = 1 TO 5
1150  IF Q1(I) < = CM THEN 1170
1160 CT(I) = XL
1170  NEXT I
1180  IF CT(M) = XL THEN 1240
1190  PRINT : PRINT
1200  PRINT "***  LIMITED INVENTORY CAPACITY   ***  "
1203  PRINT "***  IS GREATER THAN THE OPTIMAL  ***  "
1205  PRINT "***  ORDER QUANTITY; NO PROBLEM   ***  "
1207  PRINT "***  CAUSED BY LIMITATION.        ***  "
1210  PRINT : GOTO 9999: REM    END
1230  REM       EOQ WITH LIMITED CAPACITY
1240 M = 1:Q0 = Q(1):S0 = Q1(1):CT = CT(1)
1250  FOR I = 1 TO 6
1260  IF CT < = CT(I) THEN 1280
1270 M = I:Q0 = Q(I):S0 = Q1(I):CT = CT(I)
1280  NEXT I
1290  GOSUB 3000: REM       OUTPUT WITH LIMITED INVENTORY CAPACITY
1300  GOTO 9999: REM    END
2500  REM       SUBROUTINE: RESULTS WITHOUT CM
2510  PRINT "RESULTS OF THE EOQ MODEL:"
2520  PRINT "------------------------------------"
2530  PRINT "OPTIMAL ORDER QUANTITY = "; FN B(Q0);" UNITS."
2540  IF CR = 0 THEN 2560
2550  PRINT "OPTIMAL INVENTORY      = "; FN B(S0);" UNITS."
2560  PRINT "UNIT PURCHASE PRICE    = $"; FN A(P(M));"."
2570  PRINT "TOTAL HOLDING COSTS    = $"; FN A(CT);"."
2580  PRINT "------------------------------------"
2590  PRINT "ORDERS SHOULD BE PLACED "; FN C(D / Q0)
```

```
2595   PRINT "TIMES PER YEAR.
2600   PRINT "---------------------------------------"
2610   PRINT : PRINT
2620   RETURN
3000   REM        SUBROUTINE: RESULTS WITH CM
3010   PRINT "INVENTORY CAPACITY IS LESS THAN OPTIMAL"
3015   PRINT "---------------------------------------"
3020   PRINT "WITH LIMITED INVENTORY CAPACITY..."
3030   GOSUB 2500
3040   PRINT "COSTS DUE TO LIMITED CAPACITY = $"; FN A(CT - T8)
3050   PRINT "---------------------------------------"
3060   IF M < > 6 THEN  GOTO 9999
3070   PRINT "*** OPTIMAL QUANTITY = MAXIMUM CAPACITY"
3080   PRINT "---------------------------------------"
3090   RETURN
9999   END
```

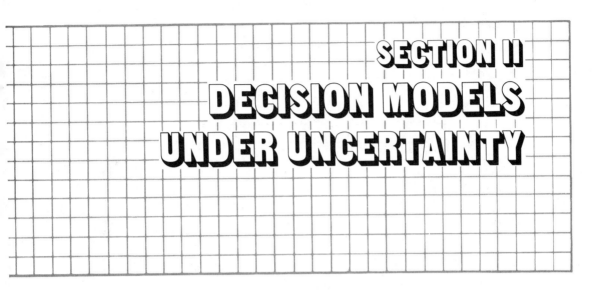

SECTION II
DECISION MODELS UNDER UNCERTAINTY

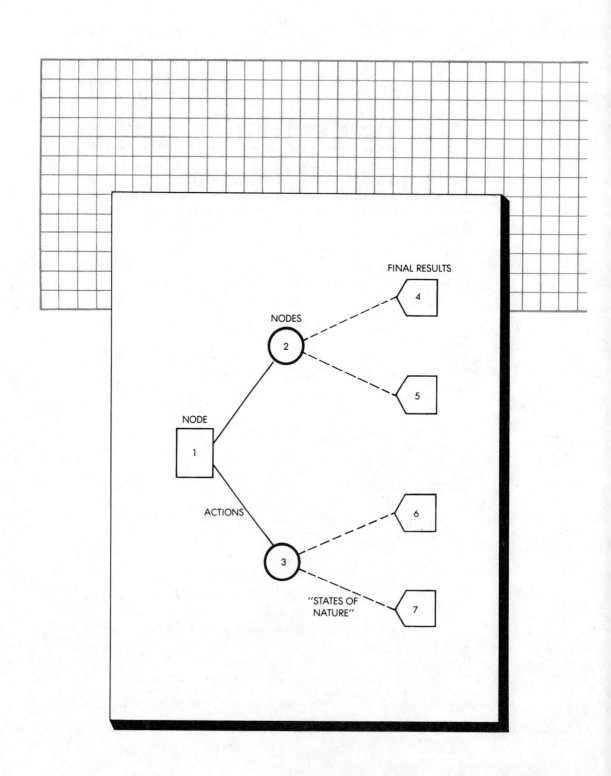

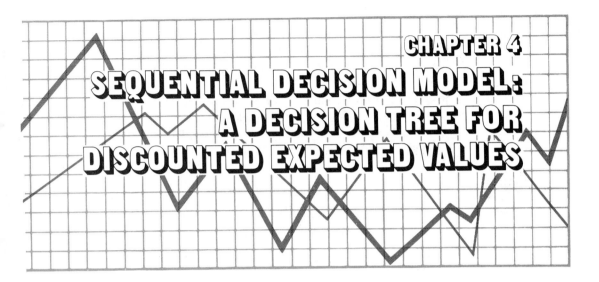

CHAPTER 4
SEQUENTIAL DECISION MODEL: A DECISION TREE FOR DISCOUNTED EXPECTED VALUES

THE METHOD

This chapter takes up one of the well-known techniques of decision-making under risk and uncertainty: the *decision tree*. The decision tree is an attempt to give formal expression to any sequential decision problem that involves risk and substantial costs or potential profits.

A *sequential decision* is actually a series of more or less interdependent decisions that are made over successive time periods. Frequently a decision made at the beginning of one period commits the decision-maker to a certain path over subsequent periods; this can mean that more profitable options are closed off by the results of an earlier decision.

By *uncertain outcomes* we mean that one present decision might lead to several different future situations, but the decision-maker cannot be sure which one will take place. To come to grips with this uncertainty, the decision-maker might consult with experts in a given field who can predict a range of *subjective probabilities* resulting from a given decision.

The decision tree is made up of *nodes* and *branches*. The nodes that represent decisions are followed by solid lines representing the resulting actions or outcomes; along each line is written the income or cost associated with that action. The nodes can also represent *external events* ("states-of-nature") that directly affect the situation under analysis; these nodes are followed by broken lines. The probability of each of these events occurring is indicated along these broken lines.

Thus when all the possible actions of a sequential decision problem have been determined, and predictions have been quantified into future probabilities, the decision tree, with its technique of calculating *expected outcomes,* can become a reasonably reliable decision tool.

THE PROGRAM

The conversational nature of this program simplifies the development of the decision tree; its output is in the form of *decision tables.* Certain rules are to be followed in using this program:

1. The nodes are numbered sequentially.
2. The outcome node of a branch must have a higher numerical value than the source node.
3. Each decision branch has a zero probability (or, more precisely, has no probability); probabilities are only used to describe uncertain external events.
4. Each branch representing an external event has a probability between 0 and 1. The sum of the probabilities of the branches coming from the same node must be equal to 1.

The decision tree program prints an error message if any of these procedures are not followed.

The program also has a *present value* routine. Since the outcome of a decision is not necessarily immediate, the choice among several possible actions often results in a comparison of revenues that are distributed differently in time. The time-value of money is accounted for by finding the present value of all of these future revenues (or costs). This process requires two pieces of information: the discount rate and the number of periods that will elapse before a given revenue becomes available.

The input routine of this program is in lines 80 to 340. Data input for a decision tree problem is not always easy to plan; for this reason the program contains several tests (lines 250, 270, and 290) to detect the most common errors. Drawing out the decision tree on paper in advance can simplify the use of this program.

Lines 360 to 680 present the decision tree in table form. Two sorting algorithms arrange the source and outcomes in ascending order. Before evaluation of the decision tree, lines 700 to 730 find the present value of all the financial results, and lines 740 to 900 perform a last check on the structure of the tree (numbering of the nodes, and statistical distribution).

The expected return of each state-of-nature node is determined in lines 950 to 1020. The expected return is simply the weighted sum of the values of the final results. (Each final result is weighted by its probability of occurring.)

Lines 1030 to 1260 evaluate the financial consequences of the decision branches. Evaluation of decision branches and state-of-nature branches are printed in table form by lines 1290 to 1390. Line 1320 distinguishes between the two types of evaluation in this table.

The last table produced by the program displays the optimal decisions and their expected results. This table is printed by lines 1430 to 1550.

APPLICATION EXAMPLE

The Problem

As part of its plan to modernize its fleet, International Airlines is buying six Airbus jets. This will mean that a DC-8 now in use will no longer be needed, at least in International's present flight schedule. The company is thus considering two options: sell the DC-8 now or hold onto it in anticipation of an expanded future flight schedule. International is using a decision tree as a tool to analyze its options.

The Data

International can sell its DC-8 for $2 million this year, or $1.9 million next year. If the company decides to keep the jet for the moment, it will begin market research that will last one year and cost $40,000. If the study indicates that continued commercial use of the DC-8 will not be profitable (40% probability) the company will then sell the jet.

On the other hand, if the results of the study favor continued use of the DC-8 (60% probability), the company will still have two choices: sell the jet or keep it for expansion of the business. If at that point International decides to continue using the jet, the profitability of its use will depend on the world economic and political climate. Based on forecasting studies, economists establish the following table of predictions:

| | State-of-Nature: World Economic/Political Situation | | |
	Strong	Average	Weak
Probability	35%	55%	10%
Expected revenues* (in millions of $)	6	5	−3 (loss)

*from the DC-8 after two years of expansion (following the year-long market research)

The Results

See the output of our example. The table "Sorted Decision Tree" simply reproduces the input with the decision modes in ascending order, allowing examination of the original values. The second table, "Evaluation of the Decision Tree," reports the present value of the income or cost associated with each branch of the tree. It also gives the *weighted average* value of the decision to use the jet for future expansion (node 4 to node 6).

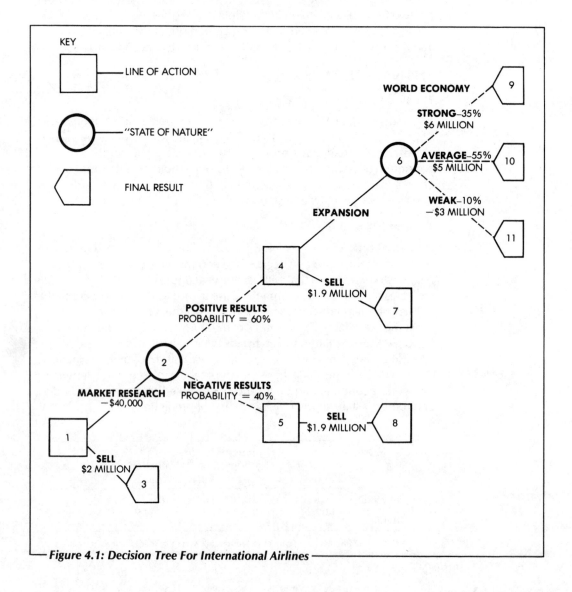

Figure 4.1: Decision Tree For International Airlines

The third table shows the best solution for each level of decision (there were three in this problem). Between "use for expansion" (node 4 to node 6) and "sell" (node 4 to node 7) the former solution is the more profitable. However between "market research" (node 1 to node 2) and "sell" (node 1 to node 3) the latter is by far the better in terms of present income. Based on information *presently available* (i.e., before taking the risk of conducting the market research) the conservative decision might be to sell the DC-8 as soon as possible; however, this decision would close off a later, more profitable option involving future expansion of the business.

The Output

```
DECISION TREE
-------------


ADJUSTMENT FOR PRESENT VALUE
YES (1) OR NO (0)? 1

DISCOUNT RATE (%)? 5


NUMBER OF BRANCHES? 10

BRANCH #1:
----------
NUMBER OF 'FROM' NODE? 1
NUMBER OF 'TO' NODE?   2
PROBABILITY? 0
ESTIMATED OUTCOME (IN $)? -40
DURATION (NUMBER OF PERIODS)? 1

BRANCH #2:
----------
NUMBER OF 'FROM' NODE? 1
NUMBER OF 'TO' NODE?   3
PROBABILITY? 0
ESTIMATED OUTCOME (IN $)? 2000
DURATION (NUMBER OF PERIODS)? 0

BRANCH #3:
----------
NUMBER OF 'FROM' NODE? 2
NUMBER OF 'TO' NODE?   4
PROBABILITY? .6
ESTIMATED OUTCOME (IN $)? 0
DURATION (NUMBER OF PERIODS)? 1

BRANCH #4:
----------
NUMBER OF 'FROM' NODE? 2
NUMBER OF 'TO' NODE?   5
PROBABILITY? .4
ESTIMATED OUTCOME (IN $)? 0
DURATION (NUMBER OF PERIODS)? 1
```

```
BRANCH #5:
-----------
NUMBER OF 'FROM' NODE? 4
NUMBER OF 'TO' NODE?   6
PROBABILITY? 0
ESTIMATED OUTCOME (IN $)? 0
DURATION (NUMBER OF PERIODS)? 1



BRANCH #6:
-----------
NUMBER OF 'FROM' NODE? 4
NUMBER OF 'TO' NODE?   7
PROBABILITY? 0
ESTIMATED OUTCOME (IN $)? 1900
DURATION (NUMBER OF PERIODS)? 1



BRANCH #7:
-----------
NUMBER OF 'FROM' NODE? 5
NUMBER OF 'TO' NODE?   8
PROBABILITY? 0
ESTIMATED OUTCOME (IN $)? 1900
DURATION (NUMBER OF PERIODS)? 1



BRANCH #8:
-----------
NUMBER OF 'FROM' NODE? 6
NUMBER OF 'TO' NODE?   9
PROBABILITY? .35
ESTIMATED OUTCOME (IN $)? 6000
DURATION (NUMBER OF PERIODS)? 3



BRANCH #9:
-----------
NUMBER OF 'FROM' NODE? 6
NUMBER OF 'TO' NODE?   10
PROBABILITY? .55
ESTIMATED OUTCOME (IN $)? 5000
DURATION (NUMBER OF PERIODS)? 3



BRANCH #10:
-----------
NUMBER OF 'FROM' NODE? 6
NUMBER OF 'TO' NODE?   11
PROBABILITY? .1
ESTIMATED OUTCOME (IN $)? -3000
DURATION (NUMBER OF PERIODS)? 3
```

```
SORTED DECISION TREE TABLE
------------------------------------------
SOURCE DEST   PROB   PERIODS   DOLLARS
------------------------------------------
  1      2     0        1       -40
  1      3     0        0       2000
  2      4    .6        1        0
  2      5    .4        1        0
  4      6     0        1        0
  4      7     0        1       1900
  5      8     0        1       1900
  6      9    .35       3       6000
  6     10    .55       3       5000
  6     11    .1        3      -3000
------------------------------------------


CONTINUE?Y


EVALUATION OF THE DECISION TREE
------------------------------------------
SOURCE DEST   PROB     PERIODS   DOLLARS
------------------------------------------
  1      2   DECISION     1      -38.1
  1      3   DECISION     0       2000
  2      4    .6          1        0
  2      5    .4          1        0
  4      6   DECISION     1      3930.46
  4      7   DECISION     1      1809.52
  5      8   DECISION     1      1809.52
  6      9    .35         3      1814.06
  6     10    .55         3      2375.55
  6     11    .1          3      -259.15
------------------------------------------


CONTINUE?Y


OPTIMAL DECISIONS RETAINED
------------------------------------------
SOURCE      DEST     EXPECTED RESULTS
------------------------------------------
  1          3          $2000
  4          6          $3930.46
  5          8          $1809.52
------------------------------------------
NOTE:
THIS TABLE SHOWS THE BEST
DECISION FOR EACH LEVEL OF
THE DECISION TREE
------------------------------------------
```

The Program Listing

```
1   REM       DECISION TREE PROGRAM
2   REM       BUI       3/81
3   REM
4   REM       VARIABLES
5   REM       AN(I)     DURATION OF DECISION
6   REM                 OR STATE-OF-NATURE
7   REM       N         NUMBER OF BRANCHES
8   REM       P(I)      NUMBER OF DESTINATION I
9   REM       S(I)      NUMBER OF SOURCE I
10  REM       PR(I)     PROBABILITY OF A STATE-OF-NATURE
11  REM       R         EXPECTED RATE OF RETURN
12  REM                 (DISCOUNT RATE)
13  REM       SO(I)     CALCULATED EXPECTED RETURN
14  REM       VA(I)     PRESENT VALUE OF RESULTS
15  REM
20  PRINT : PRINT
30  PRINT "DECISION TREE"
40  PRINT "-------------"
50  PRINT : PRINT
60  REM       DATA ENTRY
70  PRINT "ADJUSTMENT FOR PRESENT VALUE"
80  INPUT "YES (1) OR NO (0)? ";BT
90  IF BT = 0 THEN 140
100 PRINT
110 INPUT "DISCOUNT RATE (%)? ";R
120 R = R / 100
130 GOTO 150
140 R = 0
150 PRINT : PRINT
160 INPUT "NUMBER OF BRANCHES? ";N
170 IF N < 2 THEN 160
180 PRINT
190 DIM S(N + 1),P(N + 1),PR(N + 1),VA(N + 1),AN(N + 1),SO(N + 1)
200 FOR I = 1 TO N
210 PRINT "BRANCH #";I;":"
220 PRINT "-----------"
230 INPUT "NUMBER OF 'FROM' NODE? ";S(I)
240 INPUT "NUMBER OF 'TO' NODE?   ";P(I)
250 IF S(I) > = P(I) THEN 230
260 INPUT "PROBABILITY? ";PR(I)
270 IF PR(I) > 1 OR PR(I) < 0 THEN 260
280 INPUT "ESTIMATED OUTCOME (IN $)? ";VA(I)
290 IF BT < > 0 THEN 320
300 AN(I) = 0
310 GOTO 330
320 INPUT "DURATION (NUMBER OF PERIODS)? ";AN(I)
330 PRINT
340 NEXT I
350 PRINT : PRINT : PRINT
360 REM       FIRST SORT
370 FOR I = 1 TO N
380 N1 = N - 1
390 FOR J = 1 TO N1
400 IF S(J) < S(J + 1) THEN 610
410 IF S(J) > S(J + 1) THEN 450
```

```
420   REM        SECOND SORT
430   IF P(J) < P(J + 1) THEN 610
440   IF P(J) = P(J + 1) THEN 1580
450  S1 = S(J)
460  P1 = P(J)
470  TP = PR(J)
480   REM
490  TA = AN(J)
500  TV = VA(J)
510  S(J) = S(J + 1)
520  P(J) = P(J + 1)
530  PR(J) = PR(J + 1)
540  AN(J) = AN(J + 1)
550  VA(J) = VA(J + 1)
560  S(J + 1) = S1
570  P(J + 1) = P1
580  PR(J + 1) = TP
590  AN(J + 1) = TA
600  VA(J + 1) = TV
610   NEXT J,I
620   PRINT "SORTED DECISION TREE TABLE"
630   GOSUB 1650
640   FOR I = 1 TO N
650   PRINT  TAB( 2);S(I); TAB( 9);P(I); TAB( 16);PR(I);
660   PRINT  TAB( 24);AN(I); TAB( 31);VA(I)
670   NEXT I
680   GOSUB 1690
690   REM        PRESENT VALUE ROUTINE
700   FOR I = 1 TO N
710   IF AN(I) < 1 THEN 730
720  VA(I) = VA(I) * (1 / ((1 + R) ^ AN(I)))
730   NEXT I
740  J = 1
750  P2 = 0
760  S2 = S(J)
770   IF N < J THEN 850
780   REM        CHECK NODE NUMBERING
790   IF S(J) < S2 THEN 1580
800   IF S(J) > S2 THEN 850
810  P2 = P2 + PR(J)
820  J = J + 1
830   GOTO 770
840   REM        CHECK PROBABILITIES (SUM = 1)
850   IF  ABS (P2 - 1) <  = .00001 THEN 870
860   IF P2 <  > 0 THEN 1580
870  P2 = PR(J)
880  S2 = S(J)
890  J = J + 1
900   IF N >  = J THEN 770
920   FOR K = 1 TO N
930  I = (N + 1) - K
940   IF PR(I) <  = 0 THEN 1040
950   REM        STATE-OF-NATURE BRANCHES
960  SO(I) = VA(I) * PR(I)
970  J = I
980  J = J - 1
990   IF J <  = 0 THEN 1010
```

```
1000   IF S(I) <  > P(J) THEN 980
1010  SO(J) = SO(J) + SO(I)
1020   GOTO 1260
1030   REM        DECISION BRANCHES
1040  SO(I) = SO(I) + VA(I)
1050  S3 = SO(I)
1060  S2 = S(I)
1070  I1 = I
1080  J = I
1090  J = J - 1
1100   IF J <  = 0 THEN 1180
1110   IF S(I) > S(J) THEN 1180
1120   IF S(I) < S(J) THEN 1580
1130  SO(J) = SO(J) + VA(J)
1140   IF SO(J) <  = S3 THEN 1090
1150  S3 = SO(J)
1160  I1 = J
1170   GOTO 1090
1180  PR(I1) =  - 99.9
1190  K = N - J
1200   IF N <  = K THEN 1270
1210  J = (N + 1) - K
1220  J = J - 1
1230   IF J <  = 0 THEN 1250
1240   IF S2 <  > P(J) THEN 1220
1250  SO(J) = SO(J) + S3
1260   NEXT K
1270   PRINT : PRINT : PRINT
1280   INPUT "CONTINUE?";C$: PRINT : PRINT
1290   PRINT "EVALUATION OF THE DECISION TREE"
1300   GOSUB 1650
1310   FOR I = 1 TO N
1320   IF PR(I) > 0 THEN 1360
1330   PRINT  TAB( 2);S(I); TAB( 9);P(I); TAB( 13);"DECISION";
1340   PRINT  TAB( 23);AN(I); TAB( 31); INT (100 * SO(I) + .5) / 100
1350   GOTO 1380
1360   PRINT  TAB( 2);S(I); TAB( 9);P(I); TAB( 15);PR(I);
1370   PRINT  TAB( 23);AN(I); TAB( 31); INT (100 * SO(I) + .5) / 100
1380   NEXT I
1390   GOSUB 1690
1400   REM        DECISION TABLE
1410   PRINT : PRINT
1420   INPUT "CONTINUE?";C$: PRINT : PRINT
1430   PRINT "OPTIMAL DECISIONS RETAINED"
1440   PRINT "-------------------------------------"
1450   PRINT "SOURCE      DEST      EXPECTED RESULTS"
1460   PRINT "-------------------------------------"
1470   FOR J = 1 TO N
1480   IF PR(J) <  > - 99.9 THEN 1500
1490   PRINT  TAB( 2);S(J); TAB( 12);P(J); TAB( 26);"$";
1495   PRINT  INT (100 * SO(J) + .5) / 100
1500   NEXT J
1510   PRINT "-------------------------------------"
1520   PRINT "NOTE:"
1530   PRINT "THIS TABLE SHOWS THE BEST"
1540   PRINT "DECISION FOR EACH LEVEL OF"
1550   PRINT "THE DECISION TREE"
1560   PRINT "-------------------------------------"
1570   END
```

```
1580   REM        ERROR MESSAGES
1590   PRINT
1600   PRINT "ERROR IN BRANCH (";S(J);",";P(J);")"
1610   PRINT "VERIFY THE NODES AND PROBABILITIES
1620   PRINT "AND START AGAIN."
1630   PRINT
1640   GOTO 200
1650   PRINT "--------------------------------------"
1660   PRINT "SOURCE DEST    PROB   PERIODS   DOLLARS"
1670   PRINT "--------------------------------------"
1680   RETURN
1690   PRINT "--------------------------------------"
1700   RETURN
```

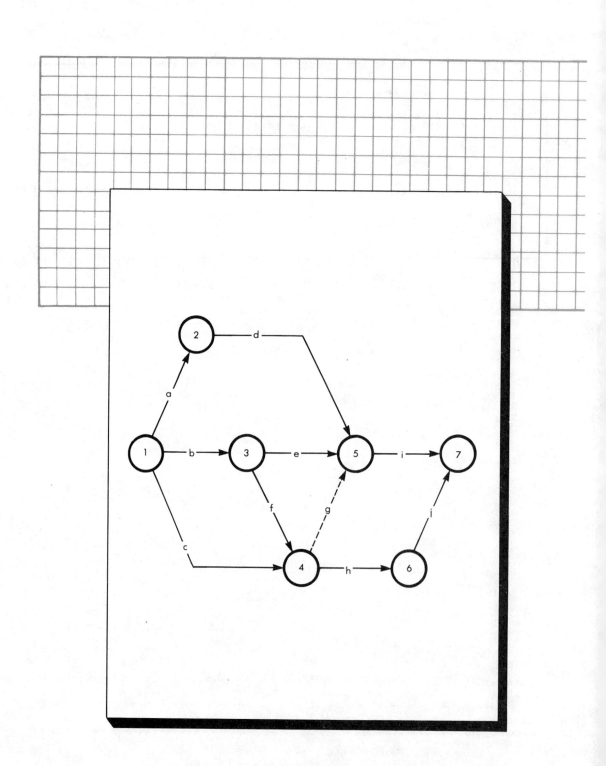

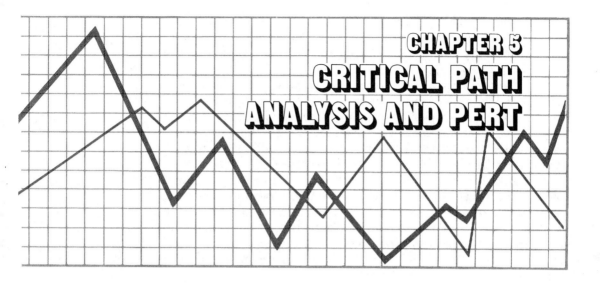

CHAPTER 5
CRITICAL PATH ANALYSIS AND PERT

THE METHOD

This chapter describes two network planning techniques that have met with success in business management—Critical Path Analysis and PERT (Program Evaluation Review Technique). These methods, which were first used in the construction industry, are now being used more and more commonly for all organizational and scheduling problems.

A *schedule* can be defined as the process of meeting a goal by accomplishing a series of tasks. The relationship between the tasks and the schedule might be *temporal* (one task cannot begin until a certain date, or must be completed by a certain date), or *sequential* (one task cannot begin until another task is completed).

Applied to this kind of problem, Critical Path Analysis can:

- identify the critical tasks, i.e., those tasks that can neither be delayed nor advanced without throwing off the schedule of the entire project.
- determine the best time frame for the project.
- establish a schedule.

PERT uses the same approach, but also calculates the uncertainty associated with the completion of the project. In projects where there are significant unknowns (new operations, for example) PERT is more effective than Critical Path Analysis.

To use these methods, we construct network diagrams made up of nodes and arrows. The nodes, which represent the events, i.e., the completion of one task and the beginning of another, are numbered in ascending order. The arrows represent the activities, or the tasks. An arrow is connected at its left to all the activities that it depends on, and, at its right, to all the activities that depend on it. The arrows are usually identified by letters; indicated along with each arrow is the amount of time needed to perform the corresponding task. (Note that the length of the arrow is not necessarily proportional to the length of the task.) If necessary, we can also draw in arrows that represent fictive tasks or ''dummy'' activities, simply to establish a continuous path to the end of the project.

When the diagram is drawn, the critical path is based on the timing of the beginning and the end of the project:

1. The *earliest starting time* for each task, from the start of the project (time = 0) to each successive node, is determined. When there are several possible paths between two points, the earliest possible starting time of the subsequent task is determined by following through the longest of the paths that lead to it.

2. The *latest finishing times* are determined by starting from the last node of the graph and deducting the amount of time necessary to complete each task.

A comparison of the earliest possible starting points and the latest completion points shows that some tasks allow *slack time* and others do not. The critical path corresponds to the earliest starting dates and the latest completion dates, i.e., the longest path between the beginning and the end of the project.

When there is uncertainty about the length of time a given task will take, PERT allows three different time estimates for each activity: the most optimistic (t_o), the most pessimistic (t_p) and the most likely (t_m) estimates. Various statistical tools can be used to estimate the probabilistic expected time (t_e) from these three figures.

Thus, critical path analysis and PERT can help to optimize the sequencing of tasks in any nonrecurring project. These tools can also aid in researching least-cost methods, either by adjustment of noncritical tasks, or by reducing the completion time of the critical tasks that can be adjusted at a reasonable expense.

THE PROGRAM

This program is the longest of the book, for two reasons: first, the PERT algorithm itself is very long; second, short instruction lines have been written to make the program more readable. The input subroutine, beginning at line 2160, contains a built-in test (line 2200) that switches the input dialogue between PERT and Critical Path Analysis.

Lines 180 to 370 sort and print the events. The **FOR/NEXT** loop in lines 400 to 450 simulates the execution time for the PERT method. Based on the three time estimates, t_o, t_p, and t_m, the formula carried out by these lines is:

$$t_e = \left(\frac{t_p + 4t_m + t_o}{6}\right) + \left(\frac{t_p - t_o}{6}\right)K$$

where

$$\frac{t_p + 4t_m + t_o}{6}$$

is the weighted average of the three time estimates,

$$\frac{t_p - t_o}{6}$$

is the standard deviation of the most optimistic and the most pessimistic estimates, and K is a random number between -1 and 1.

Thus, the formula consists of the weighted average plus or minus a random percentage of the standard deviation.

Lines 570 to 900 calculate the earliest starting times; lines 930 to 1300 calculate the latest finishing time; and lines 1320 to 1600 identify the critical path and determine the order of the path.

The following procedures must be observed in using this program:

1. The nodes are numbered in ascending order.

2. The number of the completion point of each activity must be larger than the number of the starting point.

3. Each path is completed with "dummy" activities (represented by broken lines on the path diagram) if necessary.

The program verifies these procedures and prints an error message if they are not followed.

APPLICATION EXAMPLE

The Problem

The Life and Safety Insurance Company has been studying the possibility of opening a branch office in an industrial suburb of Los Angeles. After long negotiations, Life and Safety has just signed a contract for the construction of its new office, with Clark Bernard, a local architect and contractor. In order to begin planning for its new branch (hiring personnel, conducting an advertising campaign, etc.), Life and Safety wants to know the details of the construction schedule.

The Data

With a certain amount of reticence, Bernard has compiled the following data for the construction schedule:

Activity	Estimates for Completion (in days)		
	Most Likely	Most Optimistic	Most Pessimistic
1. Architectural planning	15	9	21
2. Obtaining construction permits	30	30	45
3. Contracting	5	3	10
4. Transporting materials to site	2	2	3
5. Water and electricity installation	3	3	3
6. Foundation	10	8	15
7. Transporting soil for the garden	2	2	3
8. Walls	10	8	12
9. Roof	12	7	14
10. Landscaping	10	8	15
11. Interior design	10	9	13

The Results

See the output from the example. The program was run twice, first using Critical Path Analysis, then PERT. For both methods, the program controls the input procedure; it numbers each activity and requests the starting node, ending node, and completion time for each.

The "Schedule" tables supply the earliest starting points and the latest completion points for each task.

The "Activities" tables identify the critical tasks in the network and then display the order of the critical path. The two runs both come up with the same result: the critical path is 1, 2, 3, 4, 5, 6, 8, 9, 10, 11, which is the longest path between the beginning and the end of the project network.

The critical path analysis calculates a total project time of 95 days; PERT, taking the uncertainty into account, calculates a little more than 98 days. Thus, for the present problem the difference between the two methods is not very significant.

Hoping to reduce the total construction time, Life and Safety has requested that Bernard examine the possibilities of reducing the completion time of the critical tasks. Life and Safety is thus prepared to renegotiate some aspects of the project (labor, materials, budget) with the architect.

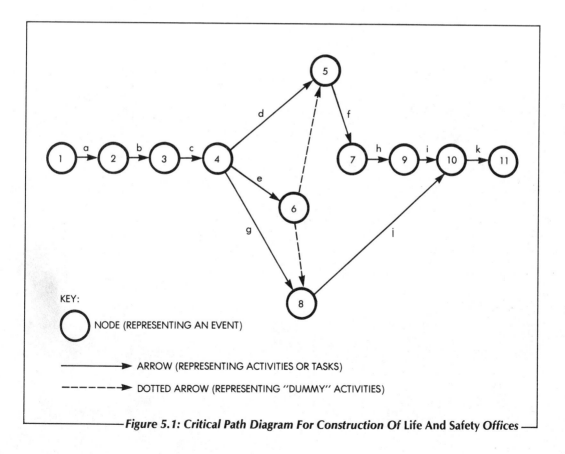

KEY:

NODE (REPRESENTING AN EVENT)

ARROW (REPRESENTING ACTIVITIES OR TASKS)

DOTTED ARROW (REPRESENTING "DUMMY" ACTIVITIES)

Figure 5.1: Critical Path Diagram For Construction Of Life And Safety Offices

---

The Output

```
CRITICAL PATH --- P.E.R.T.
-------------------------


CRITICAL PATH OR P.E.R.T. (C OR P)? C


NUMBER OF ACTIVITIES (ARROWS)? 13


ACTIVITY 1 :
DEPARTURE NODE? 1
ARRIVAL NODE?    2
LENGTH OF TASK? 15


ACTIVITY 2 :
DEPARTURE NODE? 2
ARRIVAL NODE?    3
LENGTH OF TASK? 30


ACTIVITY 3 :
DEPARTURE NODE? 3
ARRIVAL NODE?    4
LENGTH OF TASK? 5


ACTIVITY 4 :
DEPARTURE NODE? 4
ARRIVAL NODE?    6
LENGTH OF TASK? 2


ACTIVITY 5 :
DEPARTURE NODE? 4
ARRIVAL NODE?    5
LENGTH OF TASK? 3


ACTIVITY 6 :
DEPARTURE NODE? 4
ARRIVAL NODE?    7
LENGTH OF TASK? 2


ACTIVITY 7 :
DEPARTURE NODE? 5
ARRIVAL NODE?    6
LENGTH OF TASK? 0


ACTIVITY 8 :
DEPARTURE NODE? 5
ARRIVAL NODE?    7
LENGTH OF TASK? 0
```

```
ACTIVITY 9 :
DEPARTURE NODE? 6
ARRIVAL NODE?    8
LENGTH OF TASK? 10


ACTIVITY 10 :
DEPARTURE NODE? 8
ARRIVAL NODE?    9
LENGTH OF TASK? 10


ACTIVITY 11 :
DEPARTURE NODE? 7
ARRIVAL NODE?    10
LENGTH OF TASK? 10


ACTIVITY 12 :
DEPARTURE NODE? 9
ARRIVAL NODE?    10
LENGTH OF TASK? 12


ACTIVITY 13 :
DEPARTURE NODE? 10
ARRIVAL NODE?    11
LENGTH OF TASK? 10


SORTED EVENTS (NODES) :
-----------------------

1 2 3 4 6 5 7 8 9 10 11



ACTIVITIES AND CORRESPONDING DURATIONS
--------------------------------------------
ACTIVITY  FROM  TO   EXPECTED COM-
                     PLETION TIME
--------------------------------------------
   1       1    2         15
   2       2    3         30
   3       3    4          5
   4       4    6          2
   5       4    5          3
   6       4    7          2
   7       5    6          0
   8       5    7          0
   9       6    8         10
  10       8    9         10
  11       7   10         10
  12       9   10         12
  13      10   11         10
--------------------------------------------

CONTINUE? Y
```

```
EVENTS :
----------------------------------------
            -------TIME--------
EVENT      EARLIEST     LATEST     FLOAT
----------------------------------------
   1           0           0          0
   2          15          15          0
   3          45          45          0
   4          50          50          0
   6          53          53          0
   5          53          53          0
   7          53          75         22
   8          63          63          0
   9          73          73          0
  10          85          85          0
  11          95          95          0
----------------------------------------

CONTINUE? Y


ACTIVITIES :
----------------------------------------
FROM TO  EXPECTED MAXIMUM
            TIME    TIME
----------------------------------------
 1    2     15       15   CRITICAL TASK
 2    3     30       30   CRITICAL TASK
 3    4      5        5   CRITICAL TASK
 4    6      2        3
 4    5      3        3   CRITICAL TASK
 4    7      2       25
 5    6      0        0   CRITICAL TASK
 5    7      0       22
 6    8     10       10   CRITICAL TASK
 8    9     10       10   CRITICAL TASK
 7   10     10       32
 9   10     12       12   CRITICAL TASK
10   11     10       10   CRITICAL TASK
----------------------------------------


HERE IS THE ORDER OF THE CRITICAL PATH:
----------------------------------------
1 2 3 4 5 6 8 9 10 11

WITH AN ESTIMATED LENGTH OF 95




CRITICAL PATH --- P.E.R.T.
--------------------------

CRITICAL PATH OR P.E.R.T. (C OR P)? P
NUMBER OF ACTIVITIES (ARROWS)? 13
```

```
ACTIVITY 1 :
DEPARTURE NODE? 1
ARRIVAL NODE?    2
MOST LIKELY COMPLETION TIME?        15
MOST OPTIMISTIC COMPLETION TIME?  9
MOST PESSIMISTIC COMPLETION TIME? 21

ACTIVITY 2 :
DEPARTURE NODE? 2
ARRIVAL NODE?    3
MOST LIKELY COMPLETION TIME?        30
MOST OPTIMISTIC COMPLETION TIME?  30
MOST PESSIMISTIC COMPLETION TIME? 45

ACTIVITY 3 :
DEPARTURE NODE? 3
ARRIVAL NODE?    4
MOST LIKELY COMPLETION TIME?         5
MOST OPTIMISTIC COMPLETION TIME?  3
MOST PESSIMISTIC COMPLETION TIME? 10

ACTIVITY 4 :
DEPARTURE NODE? 4
ARRIVAL NODE?    6
MOST LIKELY COMPLETION TIME?         2
MOST OPTIMISTIC COMPLETION TIME?  2
MOST PESSIMISTIC COMPLETION TIME? 3

ACTIVITY 5 :
DEPARTURE NODE? 4
ARRIVAL NODE?    5
MOST LIKELY COMPLETION TIME?         3
MOST OPTIMISTIC COMPLETION TIME?  3
MOST PESSIMISTIC COMPLETION TIME? 3

ACTIVITY 6 :
DEPARTURE NODE? 4
ARRIVAL NODE?    7
MOST LIKELY COMPLETION TIME?         2
MOST OPTIMISTIC COMPLETION TIME?  2
MOST PESSIMISTIC COMPLETION TIME? 3

ACTIVITY 7 :
DEPARTURE NODE? 5
ARRIVAL NODE?    6
MOST LIKELY COMPLETION TIME?         0

ACTIVITY 8 :
DEPARTURE NODE? 5
ARRIVAL NODE?    7
MOST LIKELY COMPLETION TIME?         0

ACTIVITY 9 :
DEPARTURE NODE? 6
ARRIVAL NODE?    8
MOST LIKELY COMPLETION TIME?        10
MOST OPTIMISTIC COMPLETION TIME?  8
MOST PESSIMISTIC COMPLETION TIME? 15
```

```
ACTIVITY 10 :
DEPARTURE NODE? 8
ARRIVAL NODE?   9
MOST LIKELY COMPLETION TIME?       10
MOST OPTIMISTIC COMPLETION TIME?  8
MOST PESSIMISTIC COMPLETION TIME? 12

ACTIVITY 11 :
DEPARTURE NODE? 7
ARRIVAL NODE?   10
MOST LIKELY COMPLETION TIME?       10
MOST OPTIMISTIC COMPLETION TIME?  8
MOST PESSIMISTIC COMPLETION TIME? 15

ACTIVITY 12 :
DEPARTURE NODE? 9
ARRIVAL NODE?   10
MOST LIKELY COMPLETION TIME?       12
MOST OPTIMISTIC COMPLETION TIME?  7
MOST PESSIMISTIC COMPLETION TIME? 14

ACTIVITY 13 :
DEPARTURE NODE? 10
ARRIVAL NODE?   11
MOST LIKELY COMPLETION TIME?       10
MOST OPTIMISTIC COMPLETION TIME?  9
MOST PESSIMISTIC COMPLETION TIME? 13

SORTED EVENTS (NODES) :
----------------------

1 2 3 4 6 5 7 8 9 10 11


ACTIVITIES AND CORRESPONDING DURATIONS
--------------------------------------


ACTIVITY  FROM  TO   EXPECTED COM-
                     PLETION TIME
-----------------------------------
   1        1    2      15
   2        2    3      32.5
   3        3    4      5.5
   4        4    6      2.17
   5        4    5      3
   6        4    7      2.17
   7        5    6      0
   8        5    7      0
   9        6    8      10.5
   10       8    9      10
   11       7    10     10.5
   12       9    10     11.5
   13       10   11     10.33
-----------------------------------

CONTINUE? Y
```

```
EVENTS :
----------------------------------------
             -------TIME--------
EVENT        EARLIEST     LATEST      FLOAT
----------------------------------------
   1            0            0          0
   2           15           15          0
   3           47.5         47.5        0
   4           53           53          0
   6           56           56          0
   5           56           56          0
   7           56           77.5       21.5
   8           66.5         66.5        0
   9           76.5         76.5        0
  10           88           88          0
  11           98.33        98.33       0
----------------------------------------

CONTINUE? Y




ACTIVITIES :
----------------------------------------
FROM TO  EXPECTED MAXIMUM
            TIME     TIME
----------------------------------------
 1    2    15        15     CRITICAL TASK
 2    3    32.5      32.5   CRITICAL TASK
 3    4    5.5       5.5    CRITICAL TASK
 4    6    2.17      3
 4    5    3         3      CRITICAL TASK
 4    7    2.17      24.5
 5    6    0         0      CRITICAL TASK
 5    7    0         21.5
 6    8    10.5      10.5   CRITICAL TASK
 8    9    10        10     CRITICAL TASK
 7   10    10.5      32
 9   10    11.5      11.5   CRITICAL TASK
10   11    10.33     10.33  CRITICAL TASK
----------------------------------------




HERE IS THE ORDER OF THE CRITICAL PATH:
----------------------------------------
1 2 3 4 5 6 8 9 10 11

WITH AN ESTIMATED LENGTH OF 98.3333334
```

The Program Listing

```
1   REM        CRITICAL PATH/PERT
2   REM        BUI        4/81
3   REM
4   REM        VARIABLES
5   REM        A           NUMBER OF ACTIVITIES
6   REM        CP(I)       CRITICAL PATH
7   REM        E(I)        EARLIEST TIME FOR EVENT I
8   REM        L(I)        LATEST TIME FOR EVENT I
9   REM        LAG(I)      FLOAT TIME (L(I) - E(I))
10  REM        N(I)        NUMBER OF EVENT I
11  REM        P(I)        SOURCE OR STARTING POINT OF EVENT I
12  REM        S(I)        DESTINATION OR ARRIVAL POINT OF EVENT I
13  REM        R(I)        NUMBER OF ACTIVITY I
14  REM        SD(I)       STANDARD DEVIATION OF EXECUTION TIME
15  REM        T(I)        ESTIMATED EXECUTION TIME
16  REM        T1(I)       MOST LIKELY ESTIMATE
17  REM        T2(I)       MOST OPTIMISTIC ESTIMATE
18  REM        T3(I)       MOST PESSIMISTIC ESTIMATE
19  REM
20  PRINT : PRINT : PRINT
30  PRINT "CRITICAL PATH --- P.E.R.T."
40  PRINT "-------------------------"
50  PRINT : PRINT : PRINT
60  INPUT "CRITICAL PATH OR P.E.R.T. (C OR P)? ";Q$
70  PRINT : PRINT : PRINT
80  INPUT "NUMBER OF ACTIVITIES (ARROWS)? ";A
90  DIM N(A + 1),E(A + 1),L(A + 1),LAG(A + 1)
100  DIM T1(A),T2(A),T3(A),T(A),SD(A)
110  DIM CP(A + 1),KL(A + 1),P(A + 1),S(A + 1),R(A + 1)
120  REM        INPUT ROUTINE : PRINT : PRINT
130  FOR I = 1 TO A
140  PRINT : PRINT "ACTIVITY ";I;" :"
150  GOSUB 2160
160  NEXT I
170  PRINT
180  REM        SORTING EVENTS
190 N1 = 0
200  FOR I = 1 TO A
210  FOR J = 1 TO N1
220  IF P(I) = N(J) GOTO 260
230  NEXT J
240 N1 = N1 + 1
250  N(N1) = P(I)
260  FOR J = 1 TO N1
270  IF S(I) = N(J) GOTO 310
280  NEXT J
290 N1 = N1 + 1
300  N(N1) = S(I)
310  NEXT I
320  REM        DISPLAY EVENTS
330  PRINT "SORTED EVENTS (NODES) : "
340  PRINT "---------------------- "
350  PRINT
360  FOR J = 1 TO N1: PRINT N(J);" ";
370  NEXT J: PRINT : PRINT : PRINT
380  IF Q$ = "C" THEN 460
```

```
390  REM        CALCULATE RANDOM LENGTHS (PERT)
400   FOR I = 1 TO A
410  T(I) = (T2(I) + (4 * T1(I)) + T3(I)) / 6
420  SD(I) = (T3(I) - T2(I)) / 6
430  KI = 2 *  RND (1) - 1
440  T(I) = T(I) + (SD(I) * K1)
450   NEXT I
460   PRINT : PRINT
470   PRINT "ACTIVITIES AND CORRESPONDING DURATIONS"
480   PRINT "-----------------------------------"
490   PRINT "ACTIVITY   FROM   TO     EXPECTED COM-"
500   PRINT "                         PLETION TIME"
510   PRINT "-----------------------------------"
520   FOR I = 1 TO A
530   PRINT  TAB( 3);I; TAB( 12);P(I); TAB( 17);S(I);
540   PRINT  TAB( 25); INT (100 * T(I) + .5) / 100
550   NEXT I
560   PRINT "-----------------------------------"
570   REM        SORTING EVENTS IN ASCENDING ORDER
580   REM        ACCORDING TO DEPARTURE POINTS
590   FOR I = 1 TO A
600  R(I) = I
610   NEXT I
620  A1 = A
630  A1 = A1 - 1
640  A2 = 0
650   FOR I = 1 TO A1
660  K = R(I)
670  K1 = R(I + 1)
680   IF P(K) <  = P(K1) THEN 730
690  R1 = R(I)
700  R(I) = R(I + 1)
710  R(I + 1) = R1
720  A2 = 1
730   NEXT I
740   IF A2 = 1 THEN 630
750   REM        SEARCH EARLY EVENT TIME
760   FOR I = 1 TO A
770  K = R(I)
780  A3 = P(K)
790   GOSUB 1630
800  I1 = K3
810  K = R(I)
820  A3 = S(K)
830   GOSUB 1630
840  I2 = K3
850  K = R(I)
860  M = E(I1) + T(K)
870   IF E(I2) >  = M THEN 900
880  K = R(I)
890  E(I2) = E(I1) + T(K)
900   NEXT I
910   REM        ORDERING EVENTS ACCORDING TO
920   REM        DESCENDING ORDER OR ARRIVAL POINTS
930   FOR I = 1 TO A
940  R(I) = I
950  A1 = A
960  A1 = A1 - 1
970  A2 = 0
```

```
980   FOR I = 1 TO A1
990  K = R(I)
1000  K1 = R(I + 1)
1010   IF S(K) >  = S(K1) THEN 1060
1020  R1 = R(I)
1030  R(I) = R(I + 1)
1040  R(I + 1) = R1
1050  A2 = 1
1060   NEXT I
1070   IF A2 = 1 THEN 960
1080   REM       SEARCH LATE EVENT TIME
1090   FOR I = 1 TO A
1100  K = R(I)
1110  A3 = S(K)
1120   GOSUB 1630
1130  I1 = K3
1140  K = R(I)
1150  A3 = P(K)
1160   GOSUB 1630
1170  I2 = K3
1180  K = R(I)
1190  M = L(I1) + T(K)
1200   IF L(I2) >  = M THEN 1230
1210  K = R(I)
1220  L(I2) = L(I1) + T(K)
1230   NEXT I
1240  K = R(1)
1250  A3 = S(K)
1260   GOSUB 1630
1270  C = E(K3)
1280   FOR I = 1 TO N1
1290  L(I) = C - L(I)
1300   NEXT I
1310   REM       CALCULATE FLOAT TIME
1320   FOR I = 1 TO N1
1330  LAG(I) = L(I) - E(I)
1340   NEXT I
1350   REM       PRINT THE RESULTS
1360   GOSUB 1700
1370   REM       IDENTIFY THE CRITICAL PATH
1380  KK = 1
1390   FOR I = 1 TO N1
1400   IF  ABS (LAG(I)) >  = 0.01 THEN 1460
1410  LAG(I) = 0
1420  CP(KK) = N(I)
1430  KL(KK) = L(I)
1440  N4 = KK
1450  KK = KK + 1
1460   NEXT I
1470  N5 = N4 - 1
1480   FOR I = 1 TO N5
1490  I1 = I + 1
1500   FOR J = I1 TO N4
1510   IF KL(I) > KL(J) THEN 1540
1520   IF KL(I) < KL(J) THEN 1600
1530   IF CP(I) <  = CP(J) THEN 1600
1540  IT = KL(I)
1550  JT = CP(I)
1560  KL(I) = KL(J)
```

```
1570 CP(I) = CP(J)
1580 KL(J) = IT
1590 CP(J) = JT
1600  NEXT J,I
1610  GOSUB 1830
1620  END
1630  REM      CONTROL SUBROUTINE
1640  FOR J = 1 TO N1
1650 K3 = J
1660  IF N(K3) = A3 THEN 1690
1670  NEXT J
1680  PRINT : PRINT "NO ACTIVITY NUMBER ";A3
1690  RETURN
1700  REM      PRINT COMPLETION TIMES
1710  PRINT : INPUT "CONTINUE? ";C$: PRINT : PRINT
1720  PRINT "EVENTS : "
1730  PRINT "-----------------------------------"
1740  PRINT "          -------TIME--------"
1750  PRINT "EVENT     EARLIEST    LATEST    FLOAT"
1760  PRINT "-----------------------------------"
1770  FOR I = 1 TO N1
1780  PRINT "  ";N(I); TAB( 13); INT (100 * E(I) + .5) / 100;
1785  PRINT  TAB( 25); INT (100 * L(I) + .5) / 100;
1790  PRINT  TAB( 35); INT (100 * LAG(I) + .5) / 100
1800  NEXT I
1810  PRINT "-----------------------------------"
1820  RETURN
1830  REM      PRINT THE CRITICAL PATH AND THE COMPLETION TIMES
1840  PRINT : INPUT "CONTINUE? ";C$
1850 T5 = 0: PRINT : PRINT
1860  PRINT "ACTIVITIES : "
1870  PRINT "-----------------------------------"
1880  PRINT "FROM TO  EXPECTED MAXIMUM"
1890  PRINT "            TIME     TIME"
1900  PRINT "-----------------------------------"
1910  FOR I = 1 TO A
1920 A3 = P(I)
1930  GOSUB 1630
1940 I1 = K3
1950 A3 = S(I)
1960  GOSUB 1630
1970 I2 = K3
1980 D = L(I2) - E(I1)
1990  IF  ABS (T(I) - D) < 0.001 THEN 2030
2000  PRINT P(I); TAB( 6);S(I); TAB( 11);
2010  PRINT  INT (100 * T(I) + .5) / 100;
2015  PRINT  TAB( 20); INT (100 * D + .5) / 100
2020  GOTO 2060
2030  PRINT P(I); TAB( 6);S(I); TAB( 11); INT (100 * T(I) + .5) / 100;
2040  PRINT  TAB( 20); INT (100 * D + .5) / 100;
2045  PRINT  TAB( 26);"CRITICAL TASK"
2050 T5 = T5 + T(I)
2060  NEXT I
2070  PRINT "-----------------------------------"
2080  PRINT : PRINT
2090  PRINT "HERE IS THE ORDER OF THE CRITICAL PATH:"
2100  PRINT "-----------------------------------"
2110  FOR J = 1 TO N4: PRINT CP(J);" ";
```

```
2120    NEXT J
2130    PRINT : PRINT
2140    PRINT "WITH AN ESTIMATED LENGTH OF ";T5
2150    RETURN
2160    REM        DATA ENTRY SUBROUTINE
2170    INPUT "DEPARTURE NODE? ";P(I)
2180    INPUT "ARRIVAL NODE?    ";S(I)
2190    IF P(I) > = S(I) THEN  PRINT " <ERROR> ": GOTO 2170
2200    IF Q$ = "C" THEN  INPUT "LENGTH OF TASK? ";T(I): GOTO 2280
2210    INPUT "MOST LIKELY COMPLETION TIME?        ";T1(I)
2220    REM        VERIFY FICTIVE ACTIVITIES
2230    IF T1(I) = 0 THEN T2(I) = 0:T3(I) = 0: GOTO 2280
2240    INPUT "MOST OPTIMISTIC COMPLETION TIME?  ";T2(I)
2250    IF T2(I) > T1(I) THEN  PRINT " <ERROR> ": GOTO 2240
2260    INPUT "MOST PESSIMISTIC COMPLETION TIME? ";T3(I)
2270    IF T3(I) < T1(I) THEN  PRINT " <ERROR> ": GOTO 2260
2280    RETURN
```

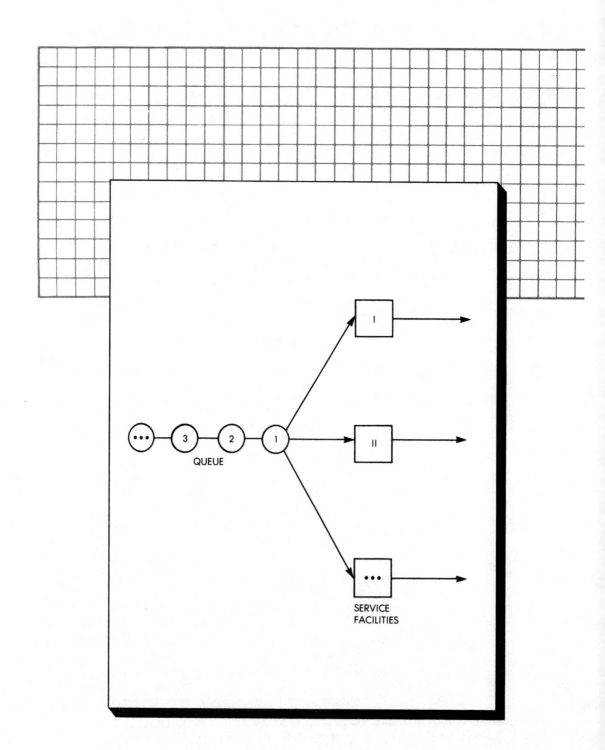

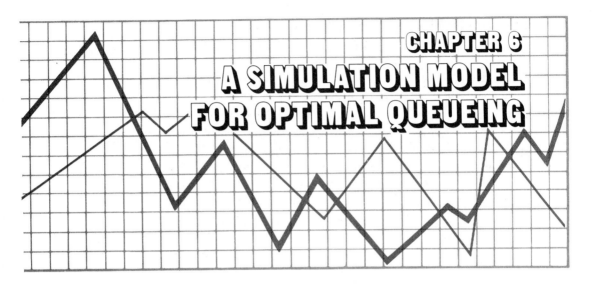

CHAPTER 6
A SIMULATION MODEL
FOR OPTIMAL QUEUEING

THE METHOD

This chapter analyzes a common simulation model used in business management: optimizing techniques for *queues,* or waiting-lines when several *service facilities* (counters, windows, cash registers, etc.) are available. Other kinds of simulation models could also be chosen for illustration, but many of them require powerful computers with large memory capacity to be implemented efficiently. The queueing model presented in this chapter, on the other hand, can be run effectively on a small computer. It analyzes a problem that is common to many businesses: waiting-lines in grocery stores, post offices, banks, stock depots, etc.

A *simulation* is a tool capable of reproducing a functional system that requires analysis, but would be extremely costly—or impossible—to study in reality. By reproducing the most important conditions of a system, a simulation allows more realistic decision making.

Applied to waiting-lines, simulation must focus on the following key elements:

1. The interval of the customers' arrival. This interval is an important factor in determining the length of the line.
2. The average length of service for each customer.
3. The number of service facilities available. The length of the wait is, of course, inversely proportional to the number of service facilities.
4. The way the line is organized. In this chapter we will examine the most general, and probably the most equitable, queue discipline— FCFS (first-come-first-served). The first customers to arrive are the first to be served.

When the interval of arrivals, the length of service, the number of service facilities, and the desired length of the simulation are specified, our simulation model evaluates the characteristics of a line: the number of customers who arrive, the number of customers served, the rate of use (over time) of each service facility, the length of the wait, and the average length of the line.

The organization of a waiting-line can directly affect the profits of a business. Reduced service may reduce personnel costs, but can end up being detrimental to the profit margin in other ways (loss of customers, tarnished reputation, production bottle-necks, etc.). On the other hand, *overly* efficient service might satisfy customers, but can prove to be too costly to the company (service available that is not really needed; unoccupied personnel). Thus it is important to consider the financial factors involved in the organization of waiting-lines.

THE PROGRAM

The simulation performed in this program assumes that all customers stand in one line, and that the first to arrive are the first served (FCFS). This is the "scenario" of the simulation; a customer faces one of three situations on arrival:

1. All the windows are occupied, and the customer stands at the back of the single line;
2. One window is free and the customer goes directly to it;
3. Several windows are free and the customer goes to one of them at random.

The program also asks the user for the maximum acceptable length of the line. This maximum length can vary considerably from one business to another; it depends not only on available space, but also on psychological factors (frustration of customers who have to wait excessively long periods).

Considering all of the factors in terms of costs (opportunity costs of waiting time, losses from unserved customers, cost of unoccupied personnel), the manager can evaluate the impact of different ways of organizing the line. A compromise must be determined that will optimize the quality of service and minimize the costs.

This program is made up of three parts. The first part (lines 30 to 250) is for input of data and initialization of variables. The input involves not only the physical aspects of the line, but also the relative costs of its operation.

The second part (lines 260 to 770) is the heart of the simulation. This single queue, multi-server model, is based on two user-created functions:

- a modular function (line 470), which is used to construct a line whose length never exceeds the specified maximum length (L5);
- a statistical function (line 500), which is used to simulate the random arrival of customers. This function follows a negative exponential distribution, particularly appropriate for a queue.

The results of these two functions go into matrix C (of order L5 × 2). This matrix stores the arrival time and the length of service for each customer. When the line is not too long (tested in line 380), the program prints the details of the queue model.

The third part of the program is financial, and is designed to help the manager make an economic and efficient decision. The costs are calculated and printed in lines 1060 to 1150.

APPLICATION EXAMPLE

The Problem

The Corner Market grocery store has been experiencing serious problems for several months now with long lines of customers on Saturdays. Customers are beginning to complain and are threatening to take their business elsewhere. Mary Gallagher, the manager of the grocery store, is worried about the problem, and wants to find a way to reduce the length of the line without losing customers.

Gallagher can think of several ways of approaching the problem:

1. Reduce the checkout time per customer by putting two employees at each cash register (one to read the prices and bag the groceries, the other to work the cash register and collect the money).

2. Reduce the checkout time by opening additional cash registers.

3. Reduce the Saturday business by persuading customers to buy their groceries on other days of the week.

Gallagher can try these approaches separately or in some combination; she wants to know what effect these measures will have on the length of the Saturday line, and on costs.

The Data

Gallagher has been gathering the following data since the beginning of the year:

1. On the average, one customer arrives every 6 seconds on Saturdays.
2. The average checkout time per customer is 42 seconds.
3. Four cash registers are in operation on Saturdays (with only one checkout clerk per register).
4. Gallagher estimates that the maximum line length that customers will put up with on Saturday is 40 persons (about 10 customers per register).

Gallagher pays her Saturday checkout clerks $3 an hour; thus, the cost of an unoccupied clerk is $.00083 per second. (The time-data for this program are all entered in seconds.) Based on complaints from customers, Gallagher estimates that opportunity costs from waiting time are $.025 per second. (When customers are discouraged by the length of the line they tend to buy fewer groceries in order to wait less time in line.) The manager of the market has also estimated the loss due to unserved customers (who go elsewhere when they see a long line) to be $.025 per second.

The Results

We should note first that the execution time for this program on a microcomputer is fairly long. For a simulation length of 1200 seconds the execution time can be up to four minutes. Also, since the results depend on a random number generator, the output from this program may vary for different computers, and for different runs.

Three runs have been performed on this simulation. The first confirms that the present situation is unacceptable. The second run, with eight cash registers open and a maximum acceptable line of 64 customers (8 per register), seems to solve the problem of the long line; however, the clerks are only busy 76% of the time. Total costs are $24.73.

The third run is an attempt to improve the efficiency rate of the clerks. By reducing the number of open registers to six, the clerks are working

95.77% of the time, a much more realistic figure. However, the loss of two cash registers lengthens the line, which in turn increases costs (mostly opportunity costs) to $181.25.

The results of the last two runs suggests that Gallagher should use more than one clerk per register to satisfy customers. Before doing so, however, she might want to run a longer simulation to obtain even more reliable results.

The Output

```
SIMULATION MODEL FOR OPTIMAL QUEUEING
--------------------------------------


LENGTH OF SIMULATION?              1200

AVERAGE INTERVAL OF ARRIVAL?       6

AVERAGE TIME OF SERVICE?           42

NUMBER OF SERVICE FACILITIES OPEN? 4

MAXIMUM ACCEPTABLE LINE LENGTH?    40

OPPORTUNITY COSTS OF WAITING TIME? .025

COST OF UNDEREMPLOYED PERSONNEL?   .00083

LOSSES FROM UNSERVED CUSTOMERS?    .025



* * * * * * * * * * * * * * * * * * * * * * * * * * * *

***   SIMULATION IN PROCESS  ***

* * * * * * * * * * * * * * * * * * * * * * * * * * * *




#######################################
         THE LINE IS TOO LONG.
         EITHER FASTER SERVICE
         OR MORE SERVICE FACILITIES
              NEEDED.

#########################################
```

```
SIMULATION MODEL FOR OPTIMAL QUEUEING
-------------------------------------


LENGTH OF SIMULATION?            1200

AVERAGE INTERVAL OF ARRIVAL?       6

AVERAGE TIME OF SERVICE?          42

NUMBER OF SERVICE FACILITIES OPEN? 8

MAXIMUM ACCEPTABLE LINE LENGTH?    64

OPPORTUNITY COSTS OF WAITING TIME? .025

COST OF UNDEREMPLOYED PERSONNEL?   .00083

LOSSES FROM UNSERVED CUSTOMERS?    .025


*****************************

***   SIMULATION IN PROCESS ***

*****************************


RESULTS OF THE SIMULATION
-------------------------

NUMBER OF CUSTOMERS ARRIVING   = 191
NUMBER OF CUSTOMERS SERVED     = 191
NUMBER OF CUSTOMERS NOT SERVED = 0


SERVICE FACILITIES:
----------------------------------------
-- WINDOW #1 SERVED 24 CUSTOMERS.
-- WINDOW #2 SERVED 24 CUSTOMERS.
-- WINDOW #3 SERVED 29 CUSTOMERS.
-- WINDOW #4 SERVED 22 CUSTOMERS.
-- WINDOW #5 SERVED 24 CUSTOMERS.
-- WINDOW #6 SERVED 25 CUSTOMERS.
-- WINDOW #7 SERVED 22 CUSTOMERS.
-- WINDOW #8 SERVED 21 CUSTOMERS.
----------------------------------------
 TOTAL EXPLOITATION = 76.0104167%
----------------------------------------


CONTINUE? Y


LINE:
----------------------------------------
-- AVERAGE LENGTH OF THE LINE : .76
-- AVERAGE LENGTH OF WAIT     : 4.78
----------------------------------------
```

```
COSTS:
------------------------------------------
-- COSTS OF UNUSED SERVICE    = 1.91
-- OPPORTUNITY COSTS          = 22.82
-- LOSS, UNSERVED CUSTOMERS   = 0
------------------------------------------
   TOTAL COSTS                = 24.73
------------------------------------------


SIMULATION MODEL FOR OPTIMAL QUEUEING
------------------------------------------

LENGTH OF SIMULATION?              1200

AVERAGE INTERVAL OF ARRIVAL?       6

AVERAGE TIME OF SERVICE?           42

NUMBER OF SERVICE FACILITIES OPEN? 6

MAXIMUM ACCEPTABLE LINE LENGTH?    48

OPPORTUNITY COSTS OF WAITING TIME? .025

COST OF UNDEREMPLOYED PERSONNEL?   .00083

LOSSES FROM UNSERVED CUSTOMERS?    .025


*****************************

***  SIMULATION IN PROCESS ***

*****************************


RESULTS OF THE SIMULATION
-------------------------

NUMBER OF CUSTOMERS ARRIVING    = 191
NUMBER OF CUSTOMERS SERVED      = 179
NUMBER OF CUSTOMERS NOT SERVED  = 12

SERVICE FACILITIES:
------------------------------------------
-- WINDOW #1 SERVED 30 CUSTOMERS.
-- WINDOW #2 SERVED 34 CUSTOMERS.
-- WINDOW #3 SERVED 33 CUSTOMERS.
-- WINDOW #4 SERVED 25 CUSTOMERS.
-- WINDOW #5 SERVED 26 CUSTOMERS.
-- WINDOW #6 SERVED 31 CUSTOMERS.
------------------------------------------
   TOTAL EXPLOITATION = 95.7777778%
------------------------------------------


CONTINUE? Y
```

```
LINE:
----------------------------------------
-- AVERAGE LENGTH OF THE LINE : 6.39
-- AVERAGE LENGTH OF WAIT     : 40.37
----------------------------------------


COSTS:
----------------------------------------
-- COSTS OF UNUSED SERVICE    = .25
-- OPPORTUNITY COSTS          = 180.7
-- LOSS, UNSERVED CUSTOMERS   = .3
----------------------------------------
   TOTAL COSTS                = 181.25
----------------------------------------
```

The Program Listing

```
1   REM       OPTIMAL QUEUEING SIMULATION
2   REM       BUI             1980
3   REM
4   REM       VARIABLES
5   REM       A         COUNTER FOR THE LENGTH
6   REM                 OF THE SIMULATION
7   REM       B         NUMBER OF CUSTOMERS SERVED
8   REM       C(L5,2)   ARRIVAL TIME AND LENGTH OF SERVICE
9   REM       C1        OPPORTUNITY COSTS FOR WAITING TIME
10  REM       C2        COST OF UNUSED SERVICE TIME
11  REM       C3        LOSS DUE TO UNSERVED CUSTOMERS
12  REM       C4        TOTAL COSTS OF UNUSED SERVICE
13  REM       C5        TOTAL OPPORTUNITY COSTS FOR WAITING TIME
14  REM       C6        TOTAL LOSS DUE TO UNSERVED CUSTOMERS
15  REM       E         NUMBER OF CUSTOMERS ARRIVING
16  REM       G         NUMBER OF SERVICE FACILITIES OPEN
17  REM       I         AVERAGE ARRIVAL INTERVAL
18  REM       J         AVERAGE DURATION OF SERVICE
19  REM       K(G)      NUMBER OF CUSTOMERS SERVED
20  REM                 AT SERVICE FACILITY G
21  REM       L         NUMBER OF UNSERVED CUSTOMERS
22  REM       L1        LENGTH OF THE LINE
23  REM       L5        MAXIMUM ACCEPTABLE LINE LENGTH
24  REM       N         LENGTH OF THE SIMULATION
25  REM       S(M)      SERVICE TIME OF
26  REM                 SERVICE FACILITY M
27  REM
28  PRINT : PRINT : PRINT
30  PRINT "SIMULATION MODEL FOR OPTIMAL QUEUEING"
40  PRINT "-------------------------------------"
50  PRINT : PRINT : PRINT
60  Z = RND ( - 1): REM       RANDOMIZE
70  REM       DATA ENTRY
80  A = 0:B = 0:E = 0:S = 0
90  INPUT "LENGTH OF SIMULATION?            ";N
```

```
100    PRINT
110    INPUT "AVERAGE INTERVAL OF ARRIVAL?      ";I
120    PRINT
130    INPUT "AVERAGE TIME OF SERVICE?          ";J
140    PRINT
150    INPUT "NUMBER OF SERVICE FACILITIES OPEN? ";G
160    PRINT
170    INPUT "MAXIMUM ACCEPTABLE LINE LENGTH?    ";L5
180    DIM C(L5,2),S(G),K(G)
190 K(M) = 0
200    PRINT
210    INPUT "OPPORTUNITY COSTS OF WAITING TIME? ";C1
220    PRINT
230    INPUT "COST OF UNDEREMPLOYED PERSONNEL?   ";C2
240    PRINT
250    INPUT "LOSSES FROM UNSERVED CUSTOMERS?    ";C3
260    REM        SIMULATION ALGORITHM
270    PRINT : PRINT : PRINT
280    PRINT "******************************"
290    PRINT
300    PRINT "***  SIMULATION IN PROCESS ***"
310    PRINT
320    PRINT "******************************"
330    PRINT : PRINT
340    REM        NEW CUSTOMER IN LINE
350    FOR T = 1 TO N
360    IF A > T THEN 580
370 E = E + 1
380    IF E - B < = L5 THEN 460
390    PRINT : PRINT : PRINT
400    PRINT "####################################"
405    PRINT
410    PRINT "          THE LINE IS TOO LONG."
420    PRINT "          EITHER FASTER SERVICE"
430    PRINT "          OR MORE SERVICE FACILITIES"
435    PRINT "              NEEDED."
437    PRINT
440    PRINT "####################################"
450    STOP
460    REM        MODULAR FUNCTION
470    DEF   FN A(X) = X - INT ((X - 1) / L5) * L5
480    REM        RANDOM NUMBER GENERATION WITH
490    REM        NEGATIVE EXPONENTIAL DISTRIBUTION.
500    DEF   FN B(X) = INT ( - X * LOG ( RND (1)) + .5)
510    REM        ARRIVAL TIME OF CUSTOMER E
520 C( FN A(E),1) = T
530    REM        SERVICE TIME FOR CUSTOMER E
540 C( FN A(E),2) =  FN B(J)
550    REM        ADJUSTING THE CLOCK FOR THE NEXT CUSTOMER
560 A = T +  FN B(I)
570    GOTO 360
580    REM        SERVICE BLOCK
590    FOR M = 1 TO G
600    IF S(M) < = T THEN 630
610    NEXT M
620    GOTO 720
630    IF B = E THEN 720
640 B = B + 1
650 S(M) = C( FN A(B),2) + T
660 K(M) = K(M) + 1
```

```
670    REM        WAITING TIME
680    T1 = T - C( FN A(B),1)
690    REM        TOTAL WAITING TIME
700    T2 = T2 + T1
710    GOTO 580
720    L = E - B
730    L1 = L1 + L
740    FOR M = 1 TO G
750    IF S(M) > T THEN S1 = S1 + 1
760    NEXT M
770    NEXT T
780    REM        OUTPUT OF RESULTS
790    PRINT : PRINT : PRINT : PRINT
800    PRINT "RESULTS OF THE SIMULATION"
810    PRINT "------------------------"
820    PRINT
830    PRINT "NUMBER OF CUSTOMERS ARRIVING    = ";E
840    PRINT "NUMBER OF CUSTOMERS SERVED      = ";B
850    PRINT "NUMBER OF CUSTOMERS NOT SERVED  = ";E - B
860    PRINT : PRINT
870    PRINT "SERVICE FACILITIES:"
880    PRINT "------------------------------------------"
890    FOR M = 1 TO G
900    PRINT "-- WINDOW #";M;" SERVED ";K(M);" CUSTOMERS."
910    NEXT M
920    PRINT "------------------------------------------"
930    PRINT " TOTAL EXPLOITATION = ";100 * S1 / (N * G);"%"
940    PRINT "------------------------------------------"
950    PRINT : PRINT
960    INPUT "CONTINUE? ";C$
970    PRINT : PRINT : PRINT
980    PRINT "LINE:"
990    PRINT "------------------------------------------"
1000    PRINT "-- AVERAGE LENGTH OF THE LINE : "; INT (100 * L1 / N) / 100
1010    PRINT "-- AVERAGE LENGTH OF WAIT     : "; INT (100 * T2 / B) / 100
1020    PRINT "------------------------------------------"
1030    PRINT : PRINT
1040    PRINT "COSTS:"
1050    PRINT "------------------------------------------"
1060    C4 =   INT (100 * ((N * G) - S1) * C2) / 100
1070    C5 =   INT (100 * T2 * C1) / 100
1080    C6 =   INT (100 * (E - B) * C3) / 100
1090    PRINT "-- COSTS OF UNUSED SERVICE     = ";C4
1100    PRINT "-- OPPORTUNITY COSTS           = ";C5
1110    PRINT "-- LOSS, UNSERVED CUSTOMERS    = ";C6
1120    REM        TOTAL COSTS
1130    PRINT "------------------------------------------"
1140    PRINT " TOTAL COSTS                   = ";C4 + C5 + C6
1150    PRINT "------------------------------------------"
1160    END
```

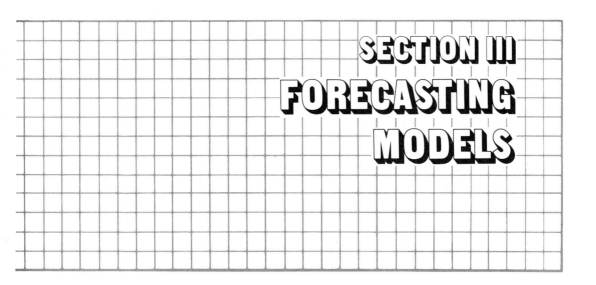

SECTION III
FORECASTING MODELS

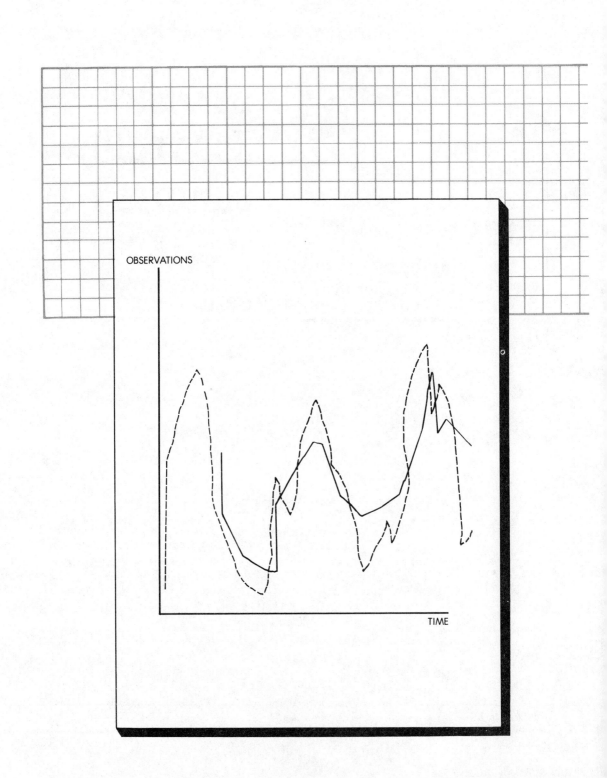

CHAPTER 7
MOVING AVERAGES

THE METHOD

The *moving average* method is a simple, short-run forecasting technique that is often used in business. Like all "smoothing" techniques, the method is based on immediate historical data. The idea is to remove unwanted fluctuations (random or otherwise) from time-series data in order to expose any trends actually represented by the data. The time series is "smoothed" by eliminating very high and very low values; a forecast can thus be based upon the intermediate values.

The moving average technique assumes that the data varies as a function of time. A moving average is thus obtained by replacing each value of the series by the average of the values that occur within a specified close range around that value. For example, a five-year moving average replaces each value of the series by the average of five years: the value itself, the two values preceeding it, and the two values following it. This method proves effective for many short-term forecasts.

Several characteristics of this method should be noted:

1. In addition to the effect of random fluctuations, the technique can separate cyclical (seasonal, monthly) fluctuations from actual trends. The number of values chosen for the calculation of the moving average is important in this respect. The number will depend on the nature of the problem being studied, but in general the period of a moving average should be equal to the period of the cyclical events that are to be smoothed from the series.

2. A number of values (equal to one-half of the period of the moving average) are lost at the beginning and the end of the time series. In our example, the program only produces 24 moving averages for 36 original data entries.

3. The moving average technique may be somewhat slow to indicate large changes in trend.

THE PROGRAM

Given a time series, the program calculates the moving averages according to the period specified by the user. The program also supplies the ratio of the original value of the time series to the calculated moving average. This ratio can aid in the forecasting task.

The program also allows multiple smoothing; it can perform the moving average technique on a series of previously smoothed data, i.e., on a series of calculated averages. With this feature, the user can further distinguish between periodic fluctuations and real trends.

The structure of this program is simple. The arithmetic mean is calculated for series of data that vary in time. These "moving" averages are calculated in lines 190 to 260. This calculation differs slightly depending on whether there is an even or odd number of periods in the base P (line 330). Lines 350 to 370 calculate the averages when P is even.

When a new set of averages is to be calculated on previously smoothed data, the arrays V (the observations), and V1 (the averages) must be reinitialized. This is done in the **FOR** loop of lines 510 to 530.

APPLICATION EXAMPLE

A union of some Wisconsin dairy farmers wants to determine an appropriate policy for production levels of butter. In advance of the next general meeting, union leaders are preparing a forecast of the demand for butter during the months ahead.

The Data

The table below shows the data available on butter consumption (in units of 10 tons) for the years 1978-1980.

Month	1978	1979	1980
Jan.	144.02	141.48	128.93
Feb.	125.17	178.47	137.30
Mar.	142.15	127.19	159.05
Apr.	153.08	142.19	154.75
May	152.27	148.43	138.11
June	131.12	149.43	140.96
July	139.43	141.18	126.49
Aug.	136.73	135.64	152.18
Sept.	136.94	144.69	149.19
Oct.	151.28	171.95	137.01
Nov.	172.20	153.60	191.35
Dec.	187.55	188.92	187.33

Because the demand for butter rises during holiday months and drops during the summer, the period used for calculating the moving averages is 12 months.

The Results

Examine the output. Since the smoothing is calculated over a 12-month period, the first six and last six months of the time series are lost. The forecast for 1981 might be presented as follows:

Jan.	148.97
Feb.	149.05
Mar.	149.92
Apr.	148.65
May	148.77
June	150.28
July	151.40
Aug.	149.16
Sept.	148.77
Oct.	150.62
Nov.	150.72
Dec.	149.93

┌─ **The Output** ─────────────────────────────────────

```
TIME-SERIES ANALYSIS
 BY MOVING AVERAGES
--------------------


NUMBER OF OBSERVATIONS? 36


VALUE FOR PERIOD 1       ?144.02
VALUE FOR PERIOD 2       ?125.17
VALUE FOR PERIOD 3       ?142.15
VALUE FOR PERIOD 4       ?153.08
VALUE FOR PERIOD 5       ?152.27
VALUE FOR PERIOD 6       ?131.12
VALUE FOR PERIOD 7       ?139.43
VALUE FOR PERIOD 8       ?136.73
VALUE FOR PERIOD 9       ?136.94
VALUE FOR PERIOD 10      ?151.28
VALUE FOR PERIOD 11      ?172.20
VALUE FOR PERIOD 12      ?187.55
VALUE FOR PERIOD 13      ?141.48
VALUE FOR PERIOD 14      ?178.47
VALUE FOR PERIOD 15      ?127.19
VALUE FOR PERIOD 16      ?142.19
VALUE FOR PERIOD 17      ?148.43
VALUE FOR PERIOD 18      ?149.43
VALUE FOR PERIOD 19      ?141.18
VALUE FOR PERIOD 20      ?135.64
VALUE FOR PERIOD 21      ?144.69
VALUE FOR PERIOD 22      ?171.95
VALUE FOR PERIOD 23      ?153.60
VALUE FOR PERIOD 24      ?188.92
VALUE FOR PERIOD 25      ?128.93
VALUE FOR PERIOD 26      ?137.30
VALUE FOR PERIOD 27      ?159.05
VALUE FOR PERIOD 28      ?154.75
VALUE FOR PERIOD 29      ?138.11
VALUE FOR PERIOD 30      ?140.96
VALUE FOR PERIOD 31      ?126.49
VALUE FOR PERIOD 32      ?152.18
VALUE FOR PERIOD 33      ?149.19
VALUE FOR PERIOD 34      ?137.01
VALUE FOR PERIOD 35      ?191.35
VALUE FOR PERIOD 36      ?187.33


MOVING AVERAGE CALCULATION
BASED ON HOW MANY PERIODS? 12


CALCULATION #1 BASED ON 12 PERIODS.
```

```
----------------------------------------
PERIOD OBSERVATION SMOOTHED VALUE RATIO
----------------------------------------
   7      139.43        147.55     .94
   8      136.73        149.67     .91
   9      136.94        151.26     .9
  10      151.28        150.18     1
  11      172.2         149.57     1.15
  12      187.55        150.17     1.24
  13      141.48        151        .93
  14      178.47        151.03     1.18
  15      127.19        151.31     .84
  16      142.19        152.5      .93
  17      148.43        152.58     .97
  18      149.43        151.87     .98
  19      141.18        151.4      .93
  20      135.64        149.16     .9
  21      144.69        148.77     .97
  22      171.95        150.62     1.14
  23      153.6         150.72     1.01
  24      188.92        149.93     1.26
  25      128.93        148.97     .86
  26      137.3         149.05     .92
  27      159.05        149.92     1.06
  28      154.75        148.65     1.04
  29      138.11        148.77     .92
  30      140.96        150.28     .93
----------------------------------------


CHANGE THE BASE PERIOD ==> TYPE <1>
CALCULATE A SECOND
    MOVING AVERAGE      ==> TYPE <2>

QUIT                    ==> TYPE <3>   ? 3
```

The Program Listing

```
1   REM       MOVING AVERAGES
2   REM       BUI        3/81
3   REM
4   REM       VARIABLES
5   REM       N           NUMBER OF PERIODS OBSERVED
6   REM       P           RANGE OF PERIODS FOR THE MOVING AVERAGES
7   REM       R           RATIO OF AVERAGE TO ORIGINAL OBSERVATION
8   REM       V(I)        OBSERVATION FOR PERIOD I
9   REM       V1(I)       MOVING AVERAGE FOR PERIOD I
10  REM
20  PRINT : PRINT : PRINT
30  PRINT "TIME-SERIES ANALYSIS"
40  PRINT " BY MOVING AVERAGES"
50  PRINT "--------------------"
55  PRINT : PRINT
```

```
60    REM        DATA INPUT
70    INPUT "NUMBER OF OBSERVATIONS? ";N
80    DIM V(N),V1(N)
90    PRINT
100   FOR I = 1 TO N
110   PRINT "VALUE FOR PERIOD ";I; TAB( 25);
120   INPUT V(I)
130   NEXT I
140 C1 = 1
150   PRINT
160   PRINT "MOVING AVERAGE CALCULATION"
170   INPUT "BASED ON HOW MANY PERIODS? ";P
180   REM        CALCULATION OF AVERAGES
190 M = N - P + 1
200   FOR I = 1 TO M
210 T = 0
220   FOR J = 1 TO P
230 T = T + V(I + J - 1)
240   NEXT J
250 V1(I) =  INT (100 * (T / P)) / 100
260   NEXT I
270   PRINT : PRINT
280   PRINT "CALCULATION #";C1;" BASED ON ";P;" PERIODS."
290   PRINT "-------------------------------------"
300   PRINT "PERIOD OBSERVATION SMOOTHED VALUE RATIO"
310   PRINT "-------------------------------------"
320 M1 = M
330   IF P <  > 2 *  INT (P / 2) THEN 380
340 M1 = M - 1
350   FOR K = 1 TO M1
360 V1(K) =  INT (100 * ((V1(K) + V1(K + 1)) / 2)) / 100
370   NEXT K
380   FOR K = 1 TO M1
390 R =  INT (100 * (V(K +  INT (P / 2)) / V1(K))) / 100
400   PRINT  TAB( 2);K +  INT (P / 2); TAB( 10);V(K +  INT (P / 2));
410   PRINT  TAB( 24);V1(K); TAB( 35);R
420   NEXT K
430   PRINT "-------------------------------------"
440   PRINT : PRINT : PRINT
450   PRINT "CHANGE THE BASE PERIOD ==> TYPE <1>"
460   PRINT "CALCULATE A SECOND"
465   PRINT "   MOVING AVERAGE        ==> TYPE <2>"
467   PRINT
470   INPUT "QUIT                     ==> TYPE <3>  ? ";C
480   ON C GOTO 150,490,550
490 C1 = C1 + 1
500 N = M1
510   FOR I = 1 TO N
520 V(I) = V1(I):V1(I) = 0
530   NEXT I
540   GOTO 150
550   END
```

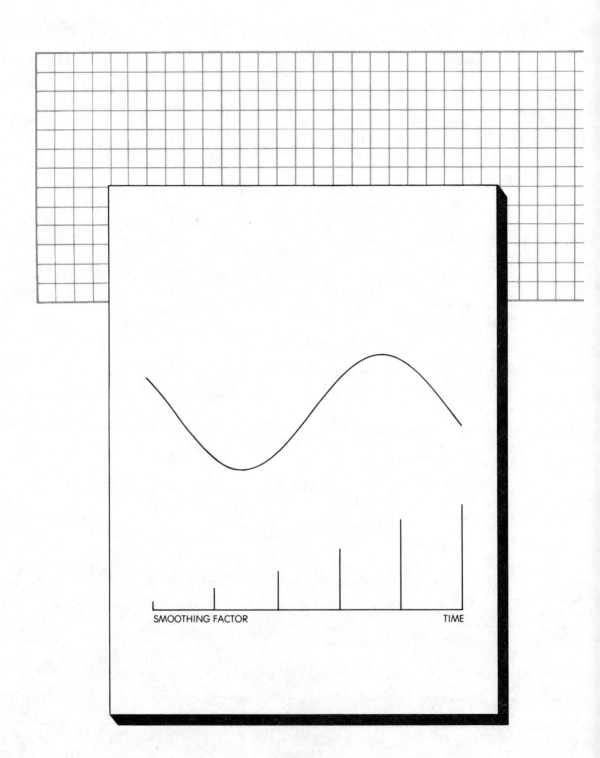

SMOOTHING FACTOR   TIME

**CHAPTER 8
EXPONENTIAL SMOOTHING**

THE METHOD

This chapter presents the *exponential smoothing* technique, which, like the moving average method, is a short-term forecasting technique based on the analysis of time-series data. Exponential smoothing uses a *weighted average* rather than the simple average calculated in the moving average method. The older the data, the less weight it is assigned in the average that produces the forecast. The *smoothing factor*, α, a value between 0 and 1, is used as a coefficient to weight each value in the time series. Since the exponent of α increases as the values go back in time, the older values become exponentially less important to the smoothed average value.

An important advantage of this method is that only two values are needed to calculate each average: the previous smoothed value, and the latest observed value of the time series. Thus there is no need to keep a record of all of the previous values of the time series.

The main difficulty of this method is that its validity rests on the choice of the smoothing constant, α. Fortunately, some methods exist, such as the *least squares technique*, that help in finding the optimal smoothing constant that most closely corresponds to the reality of the data. In many cases exponential smoothing produces reliable results, although, like the moving average, it may be slow to react to new trends.

THE PROGRAM

Based on the input time series data, this program calculates a forecast for the next period of the series, using the exponential smoothing technique. The program supplies a table of forecasts, varying α from 0.01 to 0.9. In addition, the program uses the least squares technique to determine the best smoothing constant for the forecast. Like the moving average program, this program allows the user to vary the period used to calculate the weighted average; this is particularly useful for sensitivity analysis.

The eleven α values used to compute the smoothed values are set in lines 260 to 340. The smoothed average is then computed by the subroutine at line 730. The formula represented in line 790 is the key to the exponential smoothing algorithm.

The array E stores the sum of the errors squared for each α. The minimum sum of the errors squared (and thus the best α value) is determined in lines 350 to 525.

Notice that the two α values that are not factors of 0.1 (0.01 and 0.05) require somewhat special treatment; they cannot be processed in **FOR** loops as the other α values can.

APPLICATION EXAMPLE

The Problem

Electrotime, Inc., a California manufacturing company, produces electronic watches. It buys watch casings from Switzerland. Since these parts contribute significantly to the total production costs, Electrotime wants to predict the exchange rate between the dollar and the Swiss Franc to develop a sensible reordering policy.

The Data

Electrotime has received the following average exchange rates (Swiss Francs to the dollar) for the years 1970 to 1979:

1970	4.30
1971	4.10
1972	3.81
1973	3.14
1974	2.95
1975	2.58
1976	2.49
1977	2.39
1978	1.75
1979	1.66

The Results

See the output to the program. The exponential smoothing method predicts a light rise in the rate of exchange. With $\alpha = 0.9$, the predicted exchange is 1.8. If this estimate is reliable, Electrotime should postpone reordering until the exchange rate goes up.

The Output

```
TIME SERIES ANALYSIS:
EXPONENTIAL SMOOTHING
---------------------


NUMBER OF OBSERVATIONS? 10

VALUE FOR PERIOD 1       ?4.30
VALUE FOR PERIOD 2       ?4.10
VALUE FOR PERIOD 3       ?3.81
VALUE FOR PERIOD 4       ?3.14
VALUE FOR PERIOD 5       ?2.95
VALUE FOR PERIOD 6       ?2.58
VALUE FOR PERIOD 7       ?2.49
VALUE FOR PERIOD 8       ?2.39
VALUE FOR PERIOD 9       ?1.75
VALUE FOR PERIOD 10      ?1.66

NUMBER OF PERIODS RETAINED
FOR THE SMOOTHING? 9


BEST SMOOTHING CONSTANT (ALPHA)
(DETERMINED BY FINDING THE MINIMUM OF
THE SUM OF THE ERRORS SQUARED) = .9
```

```
FORECAST FOR PERIOD 11:
-----------------------
    ALPHA       VALUE
-----------------------
    .01         3.04
    .05         2.99
    .1          2.92
    .2          2.78
    .3          2.64
    .4          2.5
    .5          2.36
    .6          2.22
    .7          2.08
    .8          1.94
    .9          1.8
-----------------------


CHANGE NUMBER OF PERIODS
RETAINED FOR THE SMOOTHING? (Y/N) N
```

The Program Listing

```
1    REM         EXPONENTIAL SMOOTHING
2    REM         BUI      3/81
3    REM
4    REM         VARIABLES
5    REM         A          CONSTANT ALPHA
6    REM         E(I)       QUADRATIC ERROR
7    REM         F          VALUE ESTIMATED BY
8    REM                    THE EXPONENTIAL SMOOTHING
9    REM         M(K)       VALUE ESTIMATED BY THE
10   REM                    EXPONENTIAL SMOOTHING FOR
11   REM                    A SPECIFIC ALPHA
12   REM         N          NUMBER OF OBSERVATIONS
13   REM         P          NUMBER OF PERIODS TO
14   REM                    BASE THE SMOOTHING ON
15   REM         V(I)       OBSERVED VALUE FOR PERIOD I
16   REM
20   PRINT : PRINT
30   PRINT "TIME SERIES ANALYSIS:"
40   PRINT "EXPONENTIAL SMOOTHING"
50   PRINT "---------------------"
60   PRINT : PRINT
70   INPUT "NUMBER OF OBSERVATIONS? ";N
80   DIM V(100),M(20),E(20)
90   PRINT
100  FOR I = 1 TO N
110  PRINT "VALUE FOR PERIOD ";I; TAB( 25);
120  INPUT V(I)
130  NEXT I
140  PRINT
150  PRINT "NUMBER OF PERIODS RETAINED"
155  INPUT "FOR THE SMOOTHING? ";P
```

```
160   REM       CALCULATION OF THE AVERAGES WITH DIFFERENT ALPHAS.
170 V1 = 0
180   IF P < 1 OR P > = N THEN 140
190   FOR I = 1 TO 10
200 M(I) = 0:E(I) = 0
210   NEXT I
220   FOR I = 1 TO P
230 V1 = V1 + V(I)
240   NEXT I
250 V2 = V1 / P
260 A = 0.01:I4 = 2
270   GOSUB 730
280 A = 0.05:I4 = 3
290   GOSUB 730
300   FOR J = 1 TO 9
310 A = J / 10
320 I4 = 3 + J
330   GOSUB 730
340   NEXT J
350   REM       FIND THE MINIMUM SUM OF THE ERRORS SQUARED.
360 I3 = 2
370 E3 = E(2)
380   FOR I = 3 TO 12
390   IF E(I) > E3 THEN 420
400 E3 = E(I)
410 I3 = I
420   NEXT I
430   IF I3 = 3 THEN 470
440   IF I3 > 3 THEN 490
450 A = 0.01
460   GOTO 510
470 A = 0.05
480   GOTO 510
490 A = 0.1 * (I3 - 3)
500   PRINT : PRINT : PRINT
510   PRINT "BEST SMOOTHING CONSTANT (ALPHA)"
520   PRINT "(DETERMINED BY FINDING THE MINIMUM OF"
525   PRINT "THE SUM OF THE ERRORS SQUARED) = ";A
530   REM       FORECAST OF N + 1
540   PRINT : PRINT
550   PRINT "FORECAST FOR PERIOD ";N + 1;":"
560   PRINT "-----------------------"
570   PRINT "   ALPHA      VALUE"
580   PRINT "-----------------------"
585   DEF  FN A(X) =  INT (100 * X + .5) / 100
590   PRINT  TAB( 4);.01; TAB( 15); FN A(M(2))
600   PRINT  TAB( 4);.05; TAB( 15); FN A(M(3))
610   FOR I = 1 TO 9
620 A = I / 10
630 K = 3 + I
640   PRINT  TAB( 4);A; TAB( 15); FN A(M(K))
650   NEXT I
660   PRINT "-----------------------"
670   PRINT : PRINT
680   PRINT "CHANGE NUMBER OF PERIODS"
690   INPUT "RETAINED FOR THE SMOOTHING? (Y/N) ";C$
700   PRINT
710   IF  LEFT$ (C$,1) < > "N" THEN 140
720   GOTO 850
```

```
730   REM        EXPONENTIAL SMOOTHING SUBROUTINE
740   P1 = P + 1
750   E1 = 0
760   F = V2
770   FOR I = P1 TO N
780   E1 = E1 + (F - V(I)) ^ 2
790   F = A * V(I) + (1 - A) * F
800   IF I < > N THEN 830
810   M(I4) = F
820   E(I4) = E1
830   NEXT I
840   RETURN
850   END
```

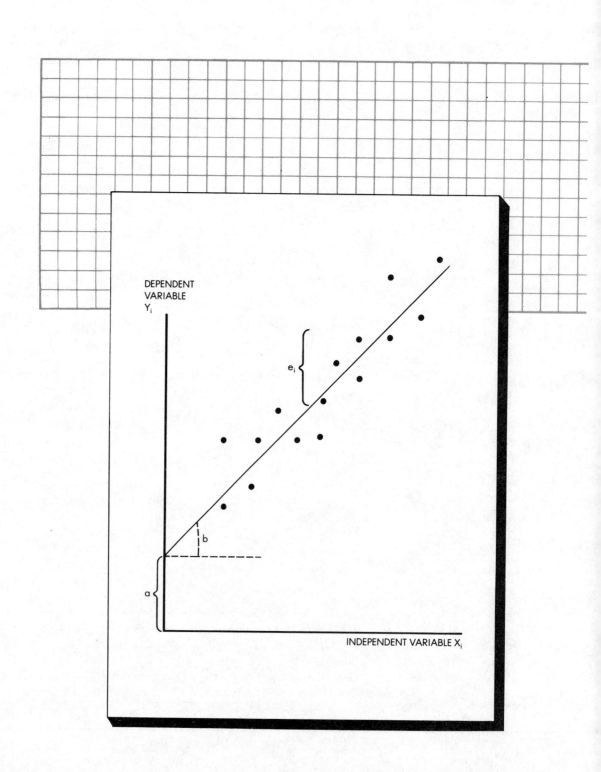

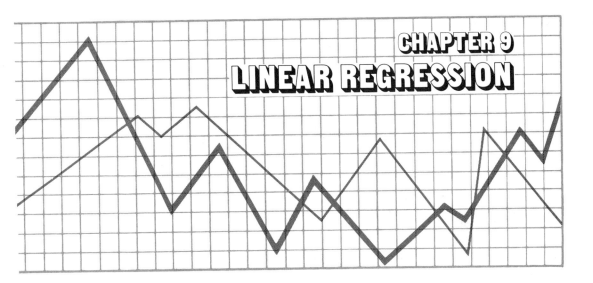

CHAPTER 9
LINEAR REGRESSION

THE METHOD

Linear regression is a method of finding the best straight-line "fit" through a set of data points. The equation for a line takes the well-known form:

$$y = a + bx$$

where x is the *independent* variable, y is the *dependent* variable, a is the *y-intercept* (the value of y when $x = 0$), and b is the *slope* of the line. This method finds the values of a and b by the least squares technique, i.e., by minimizing the sum of the residuals squared. The residual can be defined as the vertical distance between a data point and the fitted line.

Although linear regression has broader applications than the moving averages or exponential smoothing techniques, this method can also be used to analyze time series (in which case the independent variable would be time) as well as problems such as sales forecasting (using, for example, the price of the product as the independent variable and the sales volume as the dependent variable). Linear regression is often used as a predictive tool. Generally, two criteria must be met for such a use to be valid: first, the mathematical relationship must be based on a *valid theoretical model;* second, the relationship must be a relatively *stable* one. If these conditions are taken into account, linear regression can be a powerful tool for business and economics.

THE PROGRAM

Using the least-squares method, this program finds the best estimates for the linear coefficients a and b. In addition, the program determines several statistical values that can prove useful in management decisions:

1. The mean, the variance, and the standard deviation of the data.
2. Statistics that permit an evaluation of the quality of the linear fit (i.e., the statistical significance of the linear relationship): the correlation coefficient, the determination coefficient, the degrees of freedom, the standard deviation of the errors, and the test of the coefficient b (the Student test, or t-test).
3. The elasticity coefficient of the dependent variable versus the independent variable; this value gives the percentage of variation of the dependent variable when the independent variable varies by 100%.
4. The residuals, i.e., the difference between the actual data points and the calculated values of the linear fit. With this table the user can pick out any extreme values in the set of data points.

Finally, this program allows the user to request forecasts of the future behavior of the dependent variable.

The input routine, in lines 60 to 240, is clear and easy to use. By prompting the user to input names for the independent and dependent variables, the program helps avoid confusion between x and y.

The linear coefficients a and b are computed progressively in lines 260 to 450. Recall that the formulas for these coefficients (using the ordinary least squares method) are written as follows:

$$b = \frac{\Sigma xy - n\bar{x}\,\bar{y}}{\Sigma x^2 - n(\bar{x})^2}$$

$$a = \bar{y} - b\bar{x}$$

where

$$\bar{x} = \frac{1}{n}\Sigma x$$

and

$$\bar{y} = \frac{1}{n}\Sigma y$$

Thus $\bar{x}$ and $\bar{y}$ represent the *mean* of the values of x and y, respectively.

The linear curve fit equation is written explicitly, again using the names of the independent and dependent variables for clarity (lines 530 to 550). The relative value of the coefficient b (the *elasticity*) is also printed (lines

565). This value is useful for comparing linear fits having the same relational nature, but different values for x and y.

The relative statistics of the linear fit are calculated in lines 590 to 820. This routine is skipped if the number of observations, N, equals 2 (line 580). Since two points represent a line, the linear fit would be perfect and the statistical values superfluous.

The last routine of the program is devoted to prediction. It contains, in particular, a built-in path of upper and lower confidence limits (line 950). However, the path of confidence limits does not take into account the value $t_{b/2}$ of student.

APPLICATION EXAMPLE

The Problem

Hopscotch Shoes, Inc., has been marketing a new style of street shoes for the last year; the style is similar to the appearance of a running shoe. Since this is a new product, Hopscotch is keeping careful track of sales. The shoe appeals to young consumers, so the company is particularly interested in the *elasticity of demand* as the price varies.

The Data

From its eight regional sales centers, Hopscotch has gathered the following sales statistics:

Month	Units Sold	Price	Remarks
Jan.	1354	$25	product introduced
Feb.	1512	25	intensive ad campaign
Mar.	1168	35	first price hike
Apr.	987	40	second price hike
May	1030	38	
June	1100	35	
July	1426	25	summer sales
Aug.	1109	38	
Sept.	1070	40	
Oct.	1090	35	
Nov.	1150	30	price reduction
Dec.	1314	30	holiday sales

The Results

See the output of the program. Statistically, the results are satisfying (stable relationship between variables), and seem to correspond to the economic theory that sales fall when prices rise (valid theoretical model). Furthermore, since the elasticity is less than 1 (−0.74), the changes in demand are less than proportional to the changes in prices.

Examining the table of residual values, we can see that the advertising campaign (February) and holiday sales (December) play an important role, along with the price, in influencing sales of the shoes.

Finally, the linear fit was used to predict future sales for three different price estimates:

Price Policy	Price (in $)	Expected Sales
Status Quo	$30	1273
Reduction	25	1407
Increase	35	1139

Decision

Hopscotch is asking its accounting department to calculate the profit margins for these three forecasts before making a decision on price policy.

```
┌─The Output────────────────────────────────────

    SIMPLE LINEAR REGRESSION
    -----------------------

    NUMBER OF OBSERVATIONS? 12

    NAME OF THE
    DEPENDENT VARIABLE?   SHOES

    NAME OF THE
    INDEPENDENT VARIABLE? PRICE

    OBSERVED DATA FOR SHOES :
    * FROM PERIOD 1      ?1354
    * FROM PERIOD 2      ?1512
    * FROM PERIOD 3      ?1168
    * FROM PERIOD 4      ?987
    * FROM PERIOD 5      ?1030
    * FROM PERIOD 6      ?1100
    * FROM PERIOD 7      ?1426
    * FROM PERIOD 8      ?1109
    * FROM PERIOD 9      ?1070
    * FROM PERIOD 10     ?1090
    * FROM PERIOD 11     ?1150
    * FROM PERIOD 12     ?1314
```

```
OBSERVED DATA FOR PRICE :
*  FROM PERIOD 1       ?25
*  FROM PERIOD 2       ?25
*  FROM PERIOD 3       ?35
*  FROM PERIOD 4       ?40
*  FROM PERIOD 5       ?38
*  FROM PERIOD 6       ?35
*  FROM PERIOD 7       ?25
*  FROM PERIOD 8       ?38
*  FROM PERIOD 9       ?40
*  FROM PERIOD 10      ?35
*  FROM PERIOD 11      ?30
*  FROM PERIOD 12      ?30



RESULTS OF THE ANALYSIS:
-----------------------------------------
VARIABLE  MEAN    VARIANCE STD DEVIATION
--------  ----    -------- -------------
PRICE     33      33.64         5.8
SHOES     1192.5  28139.18    167.75
-----------------------------------------

LINEAR CURVE FIT:

SHOES = 2077.08 + (-26.81) * PRICE

            ELASTICITY = -74%
-----------------------------------------
CORRELATION COEFFICIENT = -.93
DETERMINATION COEFFICIENT = .86
T-TEST = -7.8
DEGREES OF FREEDOM = 10
STD DEVIATION OF THE ERRORS = 66.09
-----------------------------------------


CONTINUE? Y


TABLE OF RESIDUAL VALUES
-----------------------------------------
#      DEPENDENT VARIABLE     RESIDUAL
       OBSERVED  EXTRAPOLATED
       --------  ------------
1      1354      1406.94       52.94
2      1512      1406.94      -105.06
3      1168      1138.89      -29.11
4      987       1004.86       17.86
5      1030      1058.47       28.47
6      1100      1138.89       38.89
7      1426      1406.94      -19.06
8      1109      1058.47      -50.53
9      1070      1004.86      -65.14
10     1090      1138.89       48.89
11     1150      1272.92      122.92
12     1314      1272.92      -41.08
-----------------------------------------
SUM OF THE ERRORS SQUARED = 43674.99
-----------------------------------------
```

```
FORECAST FOR THE NEXT PERIOD? (Y/N) Y
VALUE OF THE PRICE VARIABLE
    FOR PERIOD 13 ?30

*** FORECAST FOR 'SHOES' FOR PERIOD 13:
*** SHOES = 1272.92+/-69.55 T(B/2).

ANOTHER FORECAST? (Y/N) Y
VALUE OF THE PRICE VARIABLE
    FOR PERIOD 13 ?25

*** FORECAST FOR 'SHOES' FOR PERIOD 13:
*** SHOES = 1406.94+/-74.07 T(B/2).

ANOTHER FORECAST? (Y/N) Y
VALUE OF THE PRICE VARIABLE
    FOR PERIOD 13 ?35

*** FORECAST FOR 'SHOES' FOR PERIOD 13:
*** SHOES = 1138.89+/-69.13 T(B/2).

ANOTHER FORECAST? (Y/N) N
```

The Program Listing

```
1    REM        SIMPLE LINEAR REGRESSION
2    REM        BUI             3/81
3    REM
4    REM        VARIABLES
5    REM        A, B      ESTIMATED COEFFICIENTS
6    REM        C         VALUE OF X FOR THE PERIOD N+1
7    REM        N         NUMBER OF OBSERVATIONS
8    REM        P(I)      ESTIMATED VALUES OF Y(I)
9    REM        P         PREDICTION FOR PERIOD N+1
10   REM        R         CORRELATION COEFFICIENT
11   REM        SS        SUM OF THE ERRORS SQUARED
12   REM        X(I)      OBSERVATIONS FOR THE INDEPENDENT VARIABLE
13   REM        Y(I)      OBSERVATIONS FOR THE DEPENDENT VARIABLE
14   REM
20   PRINT : PRINT
30   PRINT "SIMPLE LINEAR REGRESSION"
40   PRINT "-----------------------"
50   PRINT : PRINT
60   INPUT "NUMBER OF OBSERVATIONS? ";N
70   IF N < 2 THEN  PRINT "NUMBER MUST BE 2 OR GREATER.": GOTO 60
80   DIM Y(N),X(N),P(N)
90   PRINT
100   PRINT "NAME OF THE"
105   INPUT "DEPENDENT VARIABLE?    ";Y$
110   PRINT
120   PRINT "NAME OF THE"
125   INPUT "INDEPENDENT VARIABLE? ";X$
130   PRINT
```

```
140   PRINT "OBSERVED DATA FOR ";Y$;" :"
150   FOR I = 1 TO N
160   PRINT "* FROM PERIOD ";I; TAB( 22);
170   INPUT Y(I)
180   NEXT I
190   PRINT
200   PRINT "OBSERVED DATA FOR ";X$;" :"
210   FOR I = 1 TO N
220   PRINT "* FROM PERIOD ";I; TAB( 22);
230   INPUT X(I)
240   NEXT I
250   PRINT : PRINT : PRINT
260   T1 = 0:T2 = 0:T3 = 0:T4 = 0:T5 = 0:SS = 0
270   FOR I = 1 TO N
280   X1 = X(I) * Y(I)
290   X2 = X(I) * X(I)
300   Y2 = Y(I) * Y(I)
310   T1 = T1 + X(I)
320   T2 = T2 + Y(I)
330   T3 = T3 + X1
340   T4 = T4 + X2
350   T5 = T5 + Y2
360   NEXT I
370   M1 = T1 / N:M2 = T2 / N
380   FOR I = 1 TO N
390   V1 = (N * T4 - T1 ^ 2) / (N * (N - 1))
400   V2 = (N * T5 - T2 ^ 2) / (N * (N - 1))
410   NEXT I
420   S1 = T3 - (N * M1 * M2)
430   S2 = T4 - (N * M1 * M1)
440   S3 = T5 - (N * M2 * M2)
450   B = S1 / S2:A = M2 - (B * M1)
455   DEF  FN A(X) =  INT (100 * X + .5) / 100
460   PRINT "RESULTS OF THE ANALYSIS:"
470   PRINT "------------------------------------"
480   PRINT "VARIABLE  MEAN    VARIANCE STD DEVIATION"
490   PRINT "--------  ----    -------- -------------"
500   PRINT X$; TAB( 11); FN A(M1); TAB( 18); FN A(V1);
505   PRINT  TAB( 33); FN A( SQR (V1))
510   PRINT Y$; TAB( 11); FN A(M2); TAB( 18); FN A(V2);
515   PRINT  TAB( 33); FN A( SQR (V2))
520   PRINT "------------------------------------"
530   PRINT : PRINT "LINEAR CURVE FIT: ": PRINT
540   PRINT Y$;" = "; FN A(A);" + (";
550   PRINT  FN A(B);") * ";X$
555   PRINT
560   PRINT  TAB( 10);"ELASTICITY = ";
565   PRINT  FN A(B * (M1 / M2)) * 100;"%"
570   PRINT "------------------------------------"
580   IF N = 2 THEN 670
590   R = S1 / ( SQR (S2) *  SQR (S3))
600   PRINT "CORRELATION COEFFICIENT = "; FN A(R)
610   PRINT "DETERMINATION COEFFICIENT = "; FN A(R ^ 2)
620   PRINT "T-TEST = "; FN A((R *  SQR (N - 2)) /  SQR (1 - R ^ 2))
630   PRINT "DEGREES OF FREEDOM = "; FN A(N - 2)
640   PRINT "STD DEVIATION OF THE ERRORS = ";
645   PRINT  FN A( SQR ((S3 - B * S1) / (N - 2)))
650   PRINT "------------------------------------"
660   PRINT : PRINT
```

```
670   INPUT "CONTINUE? ";C$
680   PRINT : PRINT
690   PRINT "TABLE OF RESIDUAL VALUES"
700   PRINT "----------------------------------------"
710   PRINT "#     DEPENDENT VARIABLE    RESIDUAL"
720   PRINT "    OBSERVED  EXTRAPOLATED "
730   PRINT "   --------  ------------ "
740   REM       SUM OF THE SQUARES OF THE RESIDUALS
750   FOR I = 1 TO N
760   P(I) = A + B * X(I)
770   SS = SS + ((P(I) - Y(I)) ^ 2)
780   PRINT I; TAB( 7);Y(I); TAB( 17); FN A(P(I));
785   PRINT  TAB( 29); FN A(P(I) - Y(I))
790   NEXT I
800   PRINT "----------------------------------------"
810   PRINT "SUM OF THE ERRORS SQUARED = "; FN A(SS)
820   PRINT "----------------------------------------"
830   PRINT : PRINT
840   INPUT "FORECAST FOR THE NEXT PERIOD? (Y/N) ";C$
850   IF  LEFT$ (C$,1) = "N" THEN 990
860   PRINT "VALUE OF THE ";X$" VARIABLE "
870   PRINT "   FOR PERIOD ";N + 1;" ";
880   INPUT C
890   P = A + B * C
900   E = 1 / N + (C - M1) ^ 2 / (T4 - T1 ^ 2 / N)
910   E1 =  SQR (1 + E)
920   PRINT
930   PRINT "*** FORECAST FOR '";Y$;"'";
935   PRINT " FOR PERIOD ";N + 1;":"
940   IF N = 2 THEN  PRINT "*** ";Y$;" = "; FN A(P): GOTO 960
950   PRINT "*** ";Y$;" = "; FN A(P);"+/-";
955   PRINT  FN A(( SQR (SS / (N - 2))) * E1);" T(B/2)."
960   PRINT
970   INPUT "ANOTHER FORECAST? (Y/N) ";C$
980   IF  LEFT$ (C$,1) < > "N" THEN 860
990   END
```

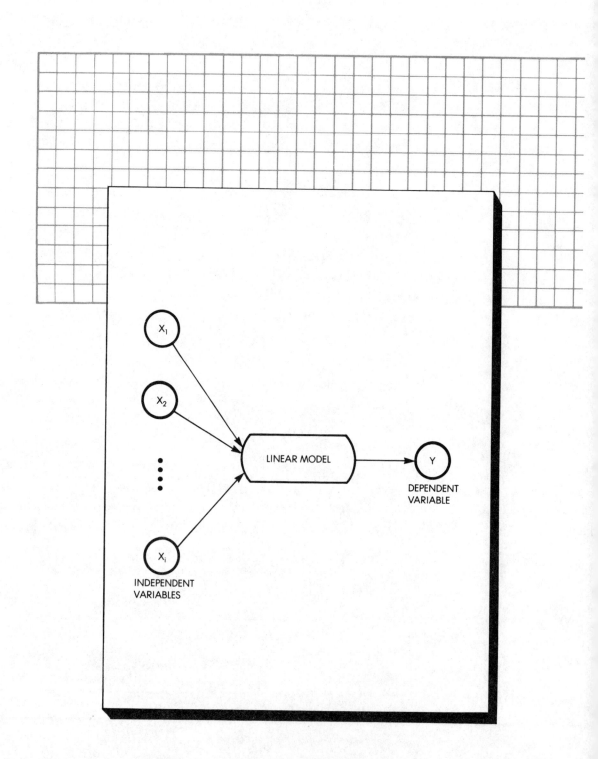

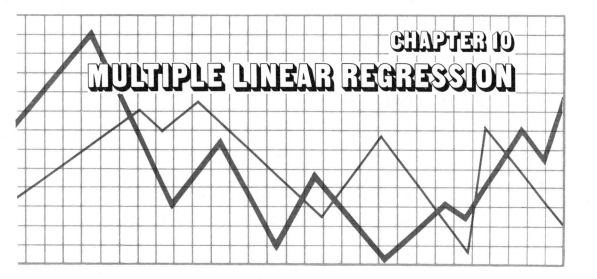

CHAPTER 10
MULTIPLE LINEAR REGRESSION

THE METHOD

Like simple linear regression, multiple linear regression is based on the least-squares method. The only difference between the two techniques is that multiple regression allows more than one independent variable. Multiple independent variables all affect the dependent variable at the same time, but often to different degrees.

Multiple regression is thus a powerful generalization of simple linear regression. It accounts for several independent factors at once, not only *quantitative* phenomena (sales levels, population growth, etc.) but also *qualitative* elements that are often essential to economic analysis (age, sex, seasonal changes, etc.). Specifically, qualitative factors often translate into *binary variables* (which take the values 0 or 1), also known as *dummy variables*.

Multiple regression is one of the most frequently used of all econometric tools. Its use in business management requires two steps:

1. Designing a model; that is, determining all of the influential factors, and analyzing the form of this influence. The construction of such a

model often borrows fundamental elements from economic theory—theories of consumption, demand, and production; marketing models; etc.

2. Determining the values of the regression coefficients. As we have already seen, the least-squares method, under its basic assumptions, gives the best estimate of these coefficients.

THE PROGRAM

Designed for general use by business managers, this program supplies a number of statistical values in addition to the linear regression equation:

1. The mean, standard deviation, and correlation matrix for the input data.
2. The statistical values that indicate the quality of the linear regression: the determination coefficient, the multiple correlation coefficient, the t-test, and the F-test.
3. The partial elasticity coefficients of the dependent variable versus each of the independent variables (expressed as percentages).
4. A table of residuals; i.e., the differences between the actual observed data and the calculated values of the linear regression.

The structure of this program resembles the program in Chapter 9; recall that both programs are based on the ordinary least-squares method. However, with two or more independent variables, the calculations are carried out in matrix form.

Notice two important characteristics of the input routine (lines 60 to 190): first, the number of variables M (introduced in line 60) must include the dependent variable; second, the data for the dependent variable are the first to be input. (In the sample run, M equals 3, for one dependent variable and two independent variables.)

Lines 200 to 420 compute the mean, variance, and standard deviation. These lines also organize the data for the calculation of the coefficients B(I) (lines 430 to 510).

The statistical tests are derived in the instructions of lines 520 to 790. Included are the determination coefficient (line 610), the Fisher test (line 630), the standard error of the estimate (line 640), and the multiple correlation coefficients (line 740). The student test is found in line 1095 (B(I)/V(I)).

Lines 950 to 1210 present a table of all the information needed for a rapid analysis of the regression equation. The statistical tests of the table verify both the quality and the stability of the regression. The estimated coefficients, and especially their relative value "beta," permit a rapid economic interpretation of the model.

APPLICATION EXAMPLE

The Problem

General Power is one of the principal electric power producers of a large western state. Because of exceptional circumstances (sharp rise in the price of petroleum, worldwide economic recession), General Power must occasionally deal with shortages, in spite of precautions and foresight.

Realizing that forecasting methods applied in the past, such as direct extrapolation of trends, are no longer relevant, General Power has engaged the services of a consulting firm specializing in forecasting research. This firm intends to base its forecast on the stable factors that influence consumption. Other, more conjectural factors, such as the effects of governmental energy policies, will be put aside for the present study.

The Data

The following information has been gathered for this example:

Year	Total Electricity Consumption GWH	Number of Domestic Users (1,000)	Personal Income (millions of $)
1960	11624	1196	11714
1961	12452	1223	12819
1962	13001	1274	13394
1963	13734	1313	14316
1964	14318	1352	15228
1965	15036	1384	15959
1966	15402	1412	16251
1967	16001	1445	16918
1968	16631	1481	17311
1969	17468	1517	18168
1970	18583	1547	19503
1971	19414	1565	21057
1972	20108	1579	21830
1973	21278	1587	22429
1974	22028	1635	22229
1975	21868	1658	21092
1976	22438	1737	20904
1977	23459	1763	21322

The Results

From the output we can formulate the following comments. The correlation matrix indicates a very strong interdependence among the variables studied. We notice in particular the strong correlation between the two independent variables introduced in the model (0.94). This suggests the eventual elimination of one of these factors—the less significant of the two—in a later study.

The results of the statistical tests on the linear regression are satisfying. We see that "number of domestic users" is a more significant variable than "personal income" (t-test). From the economic viewpoint, the regression equation shows that the increase in domestic users plays a determining role in the total electricity consumption ("domestic" elasticity = 126%) whereas the influence of income is weak ("income" elasticity = 37%).

┌─The Output ─────────────────────────────

```
MULTIPLE LINEAR REGRESSION
--------------------------



NUMBER OF VARIABLES?    3

NUMBER OF OBSERVATIONS? 18

NAME OF VARIABLE #1 ?ELECTRICITY
NAME OF VARIABLE #2 ?DOMESTIC
NAME OF VARIABLE #3 ?INCOME

DATA GATHERED FOR VARIABLE ELECTRICITY:
- PERIOD #1   ?11624
- PERIOD #2   ?12452
- PERIOD #3   ?13001
- PERIOD #4   ?13734
- PERIOD #5   ?14318
- PERIOD #6   ?15036
- PERIOD #7   ?15402
- PERIOD #8   ?16001
- PERIOD #9   ?16631
- PERIOD #10  ?17468
- PERIOD #11  ?18583
- PERIOD #12  ?19414
- PERIOD #13  ?20108
- PERIOD #14  ?21278
- PERIOD #15  ?22028
- PERIOD #16  ?21868
- PERIOD #17  ?22438
- PERIOD #18  ?23459
```

```
DATA GATHERED FOR VARIABLE DOMESTIC:
- PERIOD #1   ?1196
- PERIOD #2   ?1223
- PERIOD #3   ?1274
- PERIOD #4   ?1313
- PERIOD #5   ?1352
- PERIOD #6   ?1384
- PERIOD #7   ?1412
- PERIOD #8   ?1445
- PERIOD #9   ?1481
- PERIOD #10  ?1517
- PERIOD #11  ?1547
- PERIOD #12  ?1565
- PERIOD #13  ?1579
- PERIOD #14  ?1587
- PERIOD #15  ?1635
- PERIOD #16  ?1658
- PERIOD #17  ?1737
- PERIOD #18  ?1763

DATA GATHERED FOR VARIABLE INCOME:
- PERIOD #1   ?11714
- PERIOD #2   ?12819
- PERIOD #3   ?13394
- PERIOD #4   ?14316
- PERIOD #5   ?15228
- PERIOD #6   ?15959
- PERIOD #7   ?16251
- PERIOD #8   ?16918
- PERIOD #9   ?17311
- PERIOD #10  ?18168
- PERIOD #11  ?19503
- PERIOD #12  ?21057
- PERIOD #13  ?21830
- PERIOD #14  ?22429
- PERIOD #15  ?22229
- PERIOD #16  ?21092
- PERIOD #17  ?20904
- PERIOD #18  ?21322


CORRELATION MATRIX
------------------
1
.98      1
.96      .94       1


VARIABLE      MEAN        STD DEVIATION
---------------------------------------
ELECTRICITY   17491.2778  3784.02403
DOMESTIC      1481.55556  168.839716
INCOME        17913.5556  3517.97469


CONTINUE? Y
```

```
REGRESSION EQUATION
----------------------------------------
DEPENDENT VARIABLE: ELECTRICITY
----------------------------------------
INDEPNDNT  EST    BETA   ERRORS  T-TEST
VARIABLE   COEF   %
---------  -----  -----  ------  ------

DOMESTIC   14.93  126.43 2.29    6.52
INCOME     .36    37.26  .11     3.31
CONSTANT   -11141.8188
----------------------------------------
DETERMINATION COEFFICIENT      = .98
CORRELATION COEFFICIENT        = .99
F-TEST                         = 411.35
DEGREES OF LIBERTY             = 15
SUM OF THE ERRORS SQUARED      = 539.05
----------------------------------------


CONTINUE? Y

TABLE OF RESIDUAL VALUES
----------------------------------------
 #  OBSERVATION  ESTIMATION RESIDUAL
----------------------------------------
 1     11624      10972.91   651.09
 2     12452      11778.04   673.96
 3     13001      12748.53   252.47
 4     13734      13666.18   67.82
 5     14318      14580.19   -262.19
 6     15036      15323.85   -287.85
 7     15402      15848.05   -446.05
 8     16001      16583.35   -582.35
 9     16631      17263.71   -632.71
10     17468      18112.93   -644.93
11     18583      19046.53   -463.53
12     19414      19880.72   -466.72
13     20108      20370.99   -262.99
14     21278      20708.38   569.62
15     22028      21352.06   675.94
16     21868      21281.61   586.39
17     22438      22392.38   45.62
18     23459      22932.58   526.42
----------------------------------------
```

The Program Listing

```
1  REM      MULTIPLE LINEAR REGRESSION
2  REM      BUI              3/81
3  REM
4  REM      VARIABLES
5  REM      B(I)      ESTIMATED COEFFICIENTS
6  REM      B1        ESTIMATED CONSTANT
7  REM      C(I,J)    MULTIPLE CORRELATION COEFFICIENTS
8  REM      E         SUM OF THE ERRORS SQUARED
9  REM      F         FISHER TEST
```

```
10   REM      M          TOTAL NUMBER OF VARIABLES
11   REM      N          NUMBER OF PERIODS OF OBSERVATION
12   REM      R(I)       RESIDUAL VALUES
13   REM      R2         DETERMINATION COEFFICIENT
14   REM      S(I,J)     VARIANCE-COVARIANCE MATRIX
15   REM      V(I)       VECTOR OF STANDARD ESTIMATED ERRORS
16   REM      X(I,J)     MATRIX OF INPUT VALUES
17   REM      Y(I)       ESTIMATED Y-VALUES
18   REM
20   PRINT : PRINT : PRINT
30   PRINT "MULTIPLE LINEAR REGRESSION"
40   PRINT "-------------------------"
50   PRINT : PRINT : PRINT
60   INPUT "NUMBER OF VARIABLES?    ";M: PRINT
70   INPUT "NUMBER OF OBSERVATIONS? ";N: PRINT
80   DIM A$(M),X(M,N),X1(M),S(M,M),S2(M,M),S3(M,M)
90   DIM B(M),Y(N),R(N),V(M),C(M,M)
100  FOR I = 1 TO M: PRINT "NAME OF VARIABLE #";I;" ";
110  INPUT A$(I): NEXT I: PRINT
120  FOR I = 1 TO M
130  PRINT "DATA GATHERED FOR VARIABLE ";A$(I);":"
140  FOR J = 1 TO N
150  PRINT "- PERIOD #";J; TAB( 14);
160  INPUT X(I,J)
170  NEXT J
180  PRINT
190  NEXT I
200  REM       MEAN, STANDARD DEVIATION.
210  FOR I = 1 TO M:T = 0: FOR J = 1 TO N
220  T = T + X(I,J)
230  NEXT J
240  X1(I) = T / N
250  NEXT I
260  FOR I = 1 TO M: FOR K = 1 TO M
270  S1 = 0
280  FOR J = 1 TO N
290  S1 = S1 + (X(I,J) - X1(I)) * (X(K,J) - X1(K))
300  NEXT J
310  S(I,K) = S1 / (N - 1)
320  S(K,I) = S(I,K)
330  NEXT K,I
340  M1 = M - 1
350  FOR J = 1 TO M1: FOR K = 1 TO M1:S2(J,K) = S(J + 1,K + 1): NEXT K,J
360  FOR I = 1 TO M1: FOR J = 1 TO M1
370  IF I < > J GOTO 400
380  S3(I,J) = 1
390  GOTO 410
400  S3(I,J) = 0
410  NEXT J,I
420  GOSUB 1330
430  REM       CALCULATE THE COEFFICIENTS B(I)
440  FOR I = 1 TO M1
450  B(I) = 0
460  FOR J = 1 TO M1
470  B(I) = B(I) + S(1,J + 1) * S2(J,I)
480  NEXT J,I
490  B1 = 0
500  FOR I = 1 TO M1:B1 = B1 + X1(I + 1) * B(I): NEXT I
510  B1 = X1(1) - B1
```

```
520  REM        R2, ESTIMATIONS, SEE, F-TEST, CORRELATION
530 S3 = 0
540   FOR I = 1 TO N:Y(I) = 0
550   FOR J = 2 TO M:Y(I) = Y(I) + B(J - 1) * X(J,I): NEXT J
560 Y(I) = Y(I) + B1
570 R(I) = X(1,I) - Y(I)
580 S3 = S3 + R(I) ^ 2
590   NEXT I
600 S(1,1) = (N - 1) * S(1,1)
610 R2 = (S(1,1) - S3) / S(1,1)
620   IF R2 = 1 GOTO 640
630 F = (R2 / M1) / ((1 - R2) / (N - M))
640 E =   SQR (S3 / (N - M))
650   FOR J = 1 TO M1
660 V(J) = E *  SQR (S2(J,J) / (N - 1))
670   NEXT J
680 S(1,1) = S(1,1) / (N - 1)
690 C(1,1) = 1
700   FOR J = 2 TO M
710 C(J,J) = 1
720 J1 = J - 1
730   FOR I = 1 TO J1
740 C(I,J) = S(I,J) /  SQR (S(I,I) * S(J,J))
750 C(J,I) = C(I,J)
760   NEXT I,J
770   FOR I = 1 TO M
780 S(I,I) =   SQR (S(I,I))
790   NEXT I
800   REM        OUTPUT
810   PRINT : PRINT : PRINT
820   PRINT "CORRELATION MATRIX"
830   PRINT "------------------"
840   FOR I = 1 TO M: FOR J = 1 TO M
850   IF I < J THEN 870
860   PRINT  INT (100 * C(I,J)) / 100; TAB( 10 * J);
870   NEXT J: PRINT
880   NEXT I
890   PRINT : PRINT : PRINT
900   PRINT "VARIABLE      MEAN        STD DEVIATION"
910   PRINT "-------------------------------------"
920   FOR I = 1 TO M
923   PRINT A$(I); TAB( 14);X1(I); TAB( 27);S(I,I)
925   NEXT I
930   PRINT : PRINT
940   INPUT "CONTINUE? ";C$
950   PRINT : PRINT
960   PRINT "REGRESSION EQUATION"
970   PRINT "-------------------------------------"
990   PRINT "DEPENDENT VARIABLE: ";A$(1)
1000   PRINT "-------------------------------------"
1020   PRINT "INDEPNDNT   EST    BETA    ERRORS   T-TEST"
1030   PRINT "VARIABLE    COEF    %"
1040   PRINT "--------- -----   -----   ------   ------"
1050   PRINT
1060   FOR I = 1 TO M1
1070   PRINT A$(I + 1); TAB( 11); INT (100 * B(I) + .5) / 100; TAB( 18);
1080   PRINT  INT (10000 * (B(I) * (X1(I + 1) / X1(1)))) / 100;
1090   PRINT  TAB( 25); INT (100 * V(I) + .5) / 100;
1095   PRINT  TAB( 33); INT (100 * (B(I) / V(I)) + .5) / 100
```

```
1100    NEXT I
1110    PRINT "CONSTANT"; TAB( 11);B1
1120    PRINT "-------------------------------------"
1125    DEF  FN A(Z) =  INT (100 * Z + .5) / 100
1130    REM        STATISTICS
1140    PRINT "DETERMIANTION COEFFICIENT     = "; FN A(R2)
1150    PRINT "CORRELATION COEFFICIENT       = "; FN A( SQR (R2))
1160    PRINT "F-TEST                        = "; FN A(F)
1170    PRINT "DEGREES OF LIBERTY            = "; FN A(N - K)
1180    PRINT "SUM OF THE ERRORS SQUARED     = "; FN A(E)
1190    PRINT "-------------------------------------"
1200    REM        RESIDUALS
1210    PRINT : PRINT
1220    INPUT "CONTINUE? ";C$
1230    PRINT : PRINT
1240    PRINT "TABLE OF RESIDUAL VALUES"
1250    PRINT "-------------------------------------"
1260    PRINT " #  OBSERVATION  ESTIMATION RESIDUAL   "
1270    PRINT "-------------------------------------"
1280    FOR I = 1 TO N
1290    PRINT " ";I; TAB( 8); INT (100 * (X(1,I)) + .5) / 100;
1293    PRINT  TAB( 18); INT (100 * Y(I) + .5) / 100;
1295    PRINT  TAB( 30); INT (100 * R(I) + .5) / 100
1300    NEXT I
1310    PRINT "-------------------------------------"
1320    END
1330    REM        MATRIX INVERSION
1340    FOR K = 1 TO M1: FOR I = 1 TO M1
1350    IF I > K THEN 1420
1360    PP = S2(K,K)
1370    FOR J = 1 TO M1
1380    S2(K,J) = S2(K,J) / PP
1390    S3(K,J) = S3(K,J) / PP
1400    NEXT J
1410    IF I = K GOTO 1470
1420    PP = S2(I,K)
1430    FOR J = 1 TO M1
1440    S2(I,J) = S2(I,J) - S2(K,J) * PP
1450    S3(I,J) = S3(I,J) - S3(K,J) * PP
1460    NEXT J
1470    NEXT I
1480    NEXT K
1490    FOR I = 1 TO M1: FOR J = 1 TO M1:S2(I,J) = S3(I,J): NEXT J,I
1500    RETURN
```

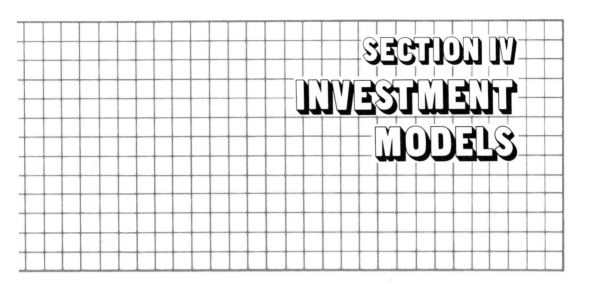

SECTION IV
INVESTMENT MODELS

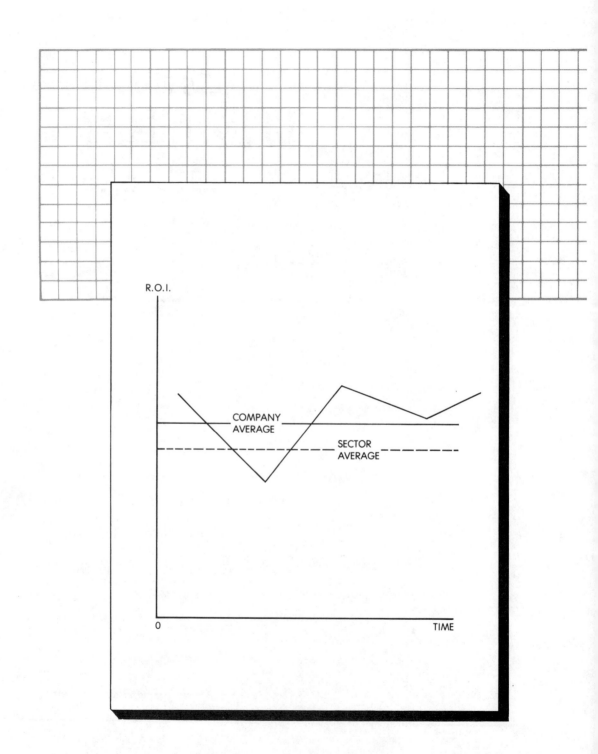

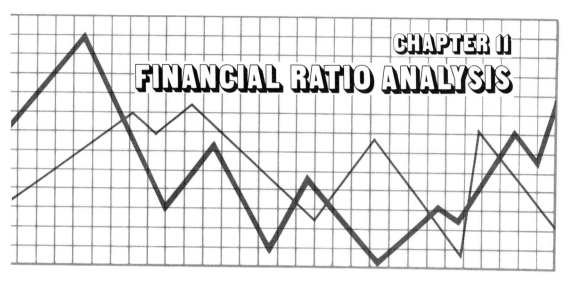

CHAPTER 11
FINANCIAL RATIO ANALYSIS

THE METHOD

Financial ratios have long been used to analyze, forecast, and control business performance. Experience has shown, however, that the analytic value of these ratios depends largely on the know-how and skill of the financial analyst. Ratios are often calculated and presented by hand, although these are tasks that can easily be performed by the computer. This chapter contains some of the most frequently used ratios, and presents a program that performs a number of the routine tasks related to ratio analysis and presentation.

The financial ratio measures the relationship between two (or more) pieces of financial information. The decision of what types of ratios to use for any given analysis depends on the specific needs of the analyst. By its nature, a ratio has only a relative sense; the real significance of ratios is found in comparison with other data. Two kinds of comparisons are commonly used: comparison with *external standards and averages,* and comparison with *internal historical data.*

External standards include ratios and averages of financial data from other similar businesses at the same point in time. Industry averages must be used somewhat cautiously, however; if variance from the average is significant, then a more profound examination of the data may be necessary.

Historical comparisons permit an analysis of ratios over time. Note that low ratios that are rising over time are often preferable to high ratios that are decreasing. Historical trend analysis is often presented graphically, as demonstrated by the output of the program in this chapter.

THE PROGRAM

This program calculates the most commonly used financial ratios from accounting data input by the user. With a subroutine that plots graphs of the change of ratios over time, this program permits the financial analyst to produce historical studies (trend analysis) or activity studies (comparisons with the sector, or with other activities within the same business).

Ten ratio calculations have been implemented in this program. These ratios are grouped into four financial categories: liquidity, leverage, management, and profitability.

Liquidity Ratios. These ratios measure a company's ability to meet its maturing short-term obligations.

$$\text{a) Current Ratio} = \frac{\text{Current Assets}}{\text{Current Liabilities}}$$

The short-term solvency of a business is proportional to the Current Ratio. Another ratio often used to measure actual liquidity is called the Quick Ratio, or Acid Test. This ratio, which refers to those assets (cash, accounts receivable, short-term investments) that can be easily converted into cash, provides a more penetrating guide to liquidity:

$$\text{b) Quick Ratio} \atop \text{(or Acid Test)} = \frac{\text{Current Assets} - \text{Inventory}}{\text{Current Liabilities}}$$

This ratio measures a company's ability to cover short-term debts without selling inventory.

Leverage Ratios. These ratios measure the role of borrowed capital or debts in the financing of the business.

$$\text{a) Debt Ratio} = \frac{\text{Total Debt}}{\text{Total Assets}}$$

In general, a business that has a low ratio of debt to assets is under little risk in a period of recession, but will realize only modest profits in a period of rapid expansion. Conversely, the business with a high rate of indebtedness is risking great losses during a period of economic crisis, but has a good chance of reaching high profits in a period of prosperity. *Leverage analysis* will reveal a balanced indebtedness ratio.

$$\text{b) Coverage Ratio} = \frac{\text{Gross Income}}{\text{Operating Expenses}}$$

This ratio indicates the degree to which a business can reduce its income without finding itself in an embarrassing financial situation.

Management or Activity Ratios.   These ratios measure the ability to use the resources available to the business. All of these ratios refer to the relationship between invested capital and sales.

$$\text{a) Inventory Turnover Ratio} = \frac{\text{Sales}}{\text{Average Inventory}}$$

A high rate of inventory turnover is a reflection of a healthy business, and also often confirms the significance of the liquidity ratio.

$$\text{b) Average Collection Period for Receivables} = \frac{\text{Average Receivables}}{\text{Average Daily Sales}}$$

Note that the figure for average daily sales is simply the annual sales divided by 360. The average collection period ratio gives the average amount of time it takes customers to pay for goods bought on credit.

$$\text{c) Fixed Assets Turnover} = \frac{\text{Sales}}{\text{Fixed Assets}}$$

The fixed assets turnover ratio indicates how well the business is profiting from its fixed assets.

$$\text{d) Total Assets Turnover} = \frac{\text{Sales}}{\text{Total Assets}}$$

This ratio shows the sales capacity of the business in relation to the total invested capital. If the ratio is inferior to the average for the sector, efforts should be made to improve sales or reduce unprofitable assets.

Profitability Ratios. Profitability ratios analyze management efficiency in terms of profits (or losses). Actually, these ratios can be calculated either in relation to sales or invested capital.

$$\text{a) Net Profit Margin} = \frac{\text{Profits After Taxes}}{\text{Net Sales}}$$

$$\text{b) Return on Total Assets} = \frac{\text{Net Profit After Taxes}}{\text{Total Assets}}$$

When financial charges are large, it is important to take them into account for this ratio.

$$\text{c) Return on Investment} = \frac{\text{Income After Taxes}}{\text{Investment}}$$
$$\text{(i.e., Owners' Equity)}$$

Developed by DuPont, this ratio combines management ratios and the profit margin. It measures the profitability of the investment.

The following financial data are necessary for the calculation of these ratios:

Assets	— short term assets
	— inventory
	— receivables
	— fixed assets
Liabilities	— current liabilities
	— long-term liabilities
	— capital stock (owners' equity)
Sales	— net total annual sales
	— gross margin on sales
	(net sales — cost of goods sold)
	— operating expenses (sales costs, administrative costs, depreciation expenses, etc.)

Tax Rate on Income

This program is written in block structure, making it easy to revise for individual needs. The ten ratios presented are of general use; however, the user can delete or add ratios easily.

The program is written in four sections:

Section 1 (lines 180 to 520): This section accepts the input data in a format that is convenient for reading the data from income statements.

Section 2 (lines 530 to 620): Some data needed for the ratio calculations must be generated from the input data. This section performs this task. For example, line 550 computes total assets as the sum of short-term assets and fixed assets.

Section 3 (lines 770 to 1230): This section prints a list of ratios for the last year of the period. Ratio analysis requires continuing yearly study; as a result, it is assumed that the user already has results from previous periods. If this is not the case, the program can easily be revised to print the ratios for all the periods. Lines 800 and 1050 should be modified as follows to form a **FOR** loop:

800 **FOR** I $=$ 1 **TO** N

   . . .

1050 **NEXT** I : **PRINT**

Section 4 (lines 1240 to 1790): This section produces graphs that illustrate the changes in each ratio over time. Visual output is often more dramatic than mere figures; thus these graphs may facilitate the analyst's task. Notice the algorithm expressed in lines 1580 to 1790. These lines adapt the scale of the graphs according to the value of the ratios and the amount of change over time. Finally, line 1750 prints several reference figures: the highest and lowest ratios, and the average of the ratios for the period covered.

APPLICATION EXAMPLE

The Problem

J. Smith is the owner and manager of an automobile parts store. Smith has been ill for a number of years, but has recently returned to his business. He wants to analyze the financial situation of his company, which has been managed by his son-in-law during the years of his illness.

Examining the books for the last several years, Smith realizes that there was a sharp rise in profits just before his illness and a continuing drop in profits during his absence, this in spite of a rise in sales. Smith intends to use financial ratios to verify his analysis.

The Data

From the financial statements (in units of $1000):

	1975	1976	1977	1978
Short-term assets	70	102	136	205.6
Inventory	34	51	85	137.6
Receivables	27.2	40.8	46.2	64.6
Fixed assets	31.8	38	42.8	38.4
Current liabilities	21.6	24.4	25.2	111.6
Long-term liabilities	10.2	7.6	6.8	6.2
Owners' equity	61.2	61.2	61.2	61.2
Annual sales	300	442	459	476
Gross margin on sales	40	88.4	91.8	95.2
Operating expenses	30	34	37.4	40.8
Tax rate	35%			

The Results

See the output from the program. The financial ratios for 1978 and the graphs comparing the ratios over the four years confirm Smith's analysis. The management ratios in particular underline the decreased capacity in inventory turnover. The profitability ratios also indicate falling business. Since sales are increasing, the decrease in profits must be the result of bad internal management of the business.

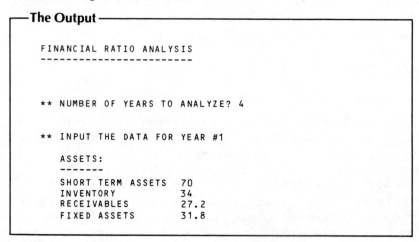

```
─The Output ─

   FINANCIAL RATIO ANALYSIS
   ------------------------


   ** NUMBER OF YEARS TO ANALYZE? 4

   ** INPUT THE DATA FOR YEAR #1

      ASSETS:
      -------
      SHORT TERM ASSETS   70
      INVENTORY           34
      RECEIVABLES         27.2
      FIXED ASSETS        31.8
```

```
       LIABILITIES:
       ------------
       CURRENT LIABILITIES    21.6
       LONG-TERM LIABILITIES  10.2
       OWNERS' EQUITY         61.2


       SALES DATA
       ----------
       TOTAL SALES            300
       GROSS MARGIN ON SALES  40
       OPERATING EXPENSES     30

**  INPUT THE DATA FOR YEAR #2

       ASSETS:
       -------
       SHORT TERM ASSETS  102
       INVENTORY          51
       RECEIVABLES        40.8
       FIXED ASSETS       38


       LIABILITIES:
       ------------
       CURRENT LIABILITIES    24.4
       LONG-TERM LIABILITIES  7.6
       OWNERS' EQUITY         61.2


       SALES DATA
       ----------
       TOTAL SALES            442
       GROSS MARGIN ON SALES  88.4
       OPERATING EXPENSES     34

**  INPUT THE DATA FOR YEAR #3

       ASSETS:
       -------
       SHORT TERM ASSETS  136
       INVENTORY          85
       RECEIVABLES        46.2
       FIXED ASSETS       42.8


       LIABILITIES:
       ------------
       CURRENT LIABILITIES    25.2
       LONG-TERM LIABILITIES  6.8
       OWNERS' EQUITY         61.2


       SALES DATA
       ----------
       TOTAL SALES            459
       GROSS MARGIN ON SALES  91.8
       OPERATING EXPENSES     37.4
```

```
** INPUT THE DATA FOR YEAR #4

   ASSETS:
   -------
   SHORT TERM ASSETS  205.6
   INVENTORY          137.6
   RECEIVABLES        64.6
   FIXED ASSETS       38.4

   LIABILITIES:
   ------------
   CURRENT LIABILITIES    111.6
   LONG-TERM LIABILITIES  6.2
   OWNERS' EQUITY         61.2

   SALES DATA
   ----------
   TOTAL SALES            476
   GROSS MARGIN ON SALES  95.2
   OPERATING EXPENSES     40.8


   TAX RATE (%) ON INCOME 35


PRINCIPAL RATIOS FOR THE LAST YEAR
----------------------------------


LIQUIDITY RATIOS
----------------
- GENERAL                 = 1.84 TIMES
- IMMEDIATE               = .61 TIMES

LEVERAGE RATIOS
----------------
- DEBTS TO ASSETS         = 48%
- COVERAGE OF COSTS       = 3.33 TIMES

MANAGEMENT RATIOS
-----------------
- INVENTORY TURNOVER      = 3.46 TIMES
- AV. COLLECTION TIME     = 49 DAYS
- FIXED ASSET TURNOVER    = 12.4 TIMES
- TOTL ASSET TURNVR       = 1.95 TIMES

PROFITABILITY RATIOS
--------------------
- PROFIT MARGIN           = 7%
- R.O.I.                  = 14%

CONTINUE? Y
GRAPHIC ANALYSIS OF RATIOS
--------------------------
LIQUIDITY RATIOS          TYPE <1>
LEVERAGE RATIOS           TYPE <2>
MANGMT RATIOS             TYPE <3>
PROFITABILITY RATIOS      TYPE <4>
NO GRAPHICS               TYPE <5>3
```

```
MANGMT RATIOS - INVENTORY TURNOVER
YEAR
    I
1   I                          *
    I
2   I                          *
    I
3   I                    *
    I
4   I              *
    I
    ------------------------------------
      -7            3            13

    1= 8.82; 2= 8.67; 3= 5.4; 4= 3.46;
    HIGH=8.82 LOW=3.46 AVERAGE=7.08

CONTINUE? Y


MANGMT RATIOS - AV. COLLECTION TIME
YEAR
    I
1   I          *
    I
2   I          *
    I
3   I             *
    I
4   I                         *
    I
    ------------------------------------
      23       33       43       53 DAYS

    1= 33; 2= 33; 3= 36; 4= 49;
    HIGH=49 LOW=33 AVERAGE=38.25

CONTINUE? Y


MANGMT RATIOS - FIXED ASSET TURNOVER
YEAR
    I
1   I               *
    I
2   I                 *
    I
3   I                *
    I
4   I                  *
    I
    ------------------------------------
      -1            9            19 TIMES

    1= 9.43; 2= 11.63; 3= 10.72; 4= 12.4;
    HIGH=12.4 LOW=9.43 AVERAGE=11.54

CONTINUE? Y
```

```
MANGMT RATIOS - TOTL ASSET TURNVR
YEAR
      I
  1   I
      I                      *
  2   I
      I                      *
  3   I
      I                       *
  4   I
      I                     *
      I
      ------------------------------------
       -9              1              11 TIMES


      1= 2.95; 2= 3.16; 3= 2.57; 4= 1.95;
      HIGH=3.16 LOW=1.95 AVERAGE=3.15



CONTINUE? Y




GRAPHIC ANALYSIS OF RATIOS
--------------------------
LIQUIDITY RATIOS            TYPE <1>
LEVERAGE RATIOS             TYPE <2>
MANGMT RATIOS               TYPE <3>
PROFITABILITY RATIOS        TYPE <4>
NO GRAPHICS                 TYPE <5>4


PROFITABILITY RATIOS - PROFIT MARGIN
YEAR
      I
  1   I
      I              *
  2   I
      I                     *
  3   I
      I                    *
  4   I
      I                   *
      I
      ------------------------------------
       -8              2              12%


      1= 2; 2= 8; 3= 8; 4= 7;
      HIGH=8 LOW=2 AVERAGE=6.75



CONTINUE? Y
```

```
        PROFITABILITY RATIOS - R.O.I.
        YEAR
             I
        1    I           *
             I
        2    I                       *
             I
        3    I                   *
             I
        4    I               *
             I
             --------------------------------
             -4        6        16        26%


             1= 6;  2= 25;  3= 20;  4= 14;
             HIGH=25 LOW=6 AVERAGE=16.75



        CONTINUE? Y



        GRAPHIC ANALYSIS OF RATIOS
        --------------------------
        LIQUIDITY RATIOS              TYPE <1>
        LEVERAGE RATIOS               TYPE <2>
        MANGMT RATIOS                 TYPE <3>
        PROFITABILITY RATIOS          TYPE <4>
        NO GRAPHICS                   TYPE <5>5
```

The Program Listing

```
1    REM      FINANCIAL ANALYSIS BY RATIOS
2    REM      BUI          1/81
3    REM
4    REM      VARIABLES
5    REM      ACT(I)   SHORT TERM ASSETS,
6    REM               PERIOD I
7    REM      AX       TOTAL ASSETS
8    REM      BAF(I)   AFTER-TAX PROFITS
9    REM      BB(I)    GROSS MARGIN ON SALES
10   REM      BNB(I)   NET INCOME BEFORE TAXES
11   REM      CP(I)    OWNERS' EQUITY
12   REM      DB(I)    RECEIVABLES
13   REM      DCT(I)   CURRENT LIABILITIES
14   REM      DET(I)   TOTAL LIABILITIES
15   REM      DLT(I)   LONG TERM LIABILITIES
16   REM      FF(I)    OPERATING EXPENSES
17   REM      IMM(I)   FIXED ASSETS
18   REM      IPT      INCOME TAX
19   REM      N        NUMBER OF YEARS TO ANALYZE
```

```
20  REM      STK(I)   INVENTORY
21  REM      VEN(I)   TOTAL SALES
22  REM      W(I)     TRANSITION ARRAY FOR GRAPHS
23  REM      RA(I)->  ARRAYS OF RATIOS
24  REM      RJ(I)    (SEE LINES 1080 TO 1220)
25  REM
26  PRINT : PRINT : PRINT
30  PRINT "FINANCIAL RATIO ANALYSIS"
40  PRINT "------------------------"
50  PRINT : PRINT : PRINT
60  REM
70  REM        INPUT DATA
80  GOSUB 180
90  REM        CALCULATE RESULTING ACCOUNTING VALUES
100  GOSUB 530
110  REM       CALCULATE THE RATIOS
120  GOSUB 630
130  REM        PRINT THE RESULTS
140  GOSUB 770
150  REM        PLOT THE GRAPHS
160  GOSUB 1240
170  END
180  REM        INPUT OF DATA
190  INPUT "** NUMBER OF YEARS TO ANALYZE? ";N
200  PRINT : PRINT
210  DIM ACT(N),STK(N),DB(N),IMM(N),DCT(N)
220  DIM DLT(N),CP(N),VEN(N),BB(N),FF(N)
230  DIM AX(N),DET(N),BNB(N),BAF(N)
240  DIM RA(N),RB(N),RC(N),RD(N),RE(N),RF(N)
250  DIM RG(N),RI(N),RJ(N)
260  FOR I = 1 TO N
270  PRINT "** INPUT THE DATA FOR YEAR #";I
280  PRINT
290  PRINT "   ASSETS:"
300  PRINT "   -------"
310  INPUT "   SHORT TERM ASSETS  ";ACT(I)
320  INPUT "   INVENTORY          ";STK(I)
330  INPUT "   RECEIVABLES        ";DB(I)
340  INPUT "   FIXED ASSETS       ";IMM(I)
350  PRINT : PRINT
360  PRINT "   LIABILITIES:"
370  PRINT "   -----------"
380  INPUT "   CURRENT LIABILITIES    ";DCT(I)
390  INPUT "   LONG-TERM LIABILITIES  ";DLT(I)
400  INPUT "   OWNERS' EQUITY         ";CP(I)
410  PRINT : PRINT
420  PRINT "   SALES DATA"
430  PRINT "   ----------"
440  INPUT "   TOTAL SALES            ";VEN(I)
450  INPUT "   GROSS MARGIN ON SALES  ";BB(I)
460  INPUT "   OPERATING EXPENSES     ";FF(I)
470  PRINT : PRINT
480  NEXT I
490  PRINT
500  INPUT "   TAX RATE (%) ON INCOME ";IPT
510  PRINT : PRINT : PRINT
520  RETURN
530  REM        CALCULATE RESULTING DATA
540  FOR I = 1 TO N
550  AX(I) = ACT(I) + IMM(I)
```

```
560 DET(I) = DCT(I) + DLT(I)
570 REM        NET PROFIT BEFORE TAXES
580 BNB(I) = BB(I) - FF(I)
590 REM        PROFIT AFTER TAXES
600 BAF(I) = BNB(I) - BNB(I) * (IPT / 100)
610 NEXT I
620 RETURN
630 REM        CALCULATE THE RATIOS
635 DEF  FN R(X) =  INT (100 * X + .5) / 100
637 DEF  FN P(X) =  INT (100 * X + .5)
640 FOR I = 1 TO N
650 RA(I) =  FN R(ACT(I) / DCT(I))
660 RB(I) =  FN R((ACT(I) - STK(I)) / DCT(I))
670 RC(I) =  FN P(DET(I) / AX(I))
680 RD(I) =  FN R((BB(I) + FF(I)) / FF(I))
690 RE(I) =  FN R(VEN(I) / STK(I))
700 RF(I) =  INT ((DB(I) / (VEN(I) / 360)) + .5)
710 RG(I) =  FN R(VEN(I) / IMM(I))
720 RH(I) =  FN R(VEN(I) / AX(I))
730 RI(I) =  FN P(BAF(I) / VEN(I))
740 RJ(I) =  FN P(BAF(I) / AX(I))
750 NEXT I
760 RETURN
770 REM         STRING INITIALIZATIONS
780 GOSUB 1080
790 REM         PRINT RESULTS FOR THE LAST YEAR.
800 I = N
810 Y = 28
820 PRINT "PRINCIPAL RATIOS FOR THE LAST YEAR"
830 PRINT "----------------------------------"
840 PRINT : PRINT
850 PRINT "LIQUIDITY RATIOS"
860 PRINT "----------------"
870 PRINT RA$; TAB( Y);"= ";RA(I);" TIMES"
880 PRINT RB$; TAB( Y);"= ";RB(I);" TIMES"
890 PRINT
900 PRINT "LEVERAGE RATIOS"
910 PRINT "---------------"
920 PRINT RC$; TAB( Y);"= ";RC(I);"%"
930 PRINT RD$; TAB( Y);"= ";RD(I);" TIMES"
940 PRINT : PRINT "MANAGEMENT RATIOS"
950 PRINT "----------------"
960 PRINT RE$; TAB( Y);"= ";RE(I);" TIMES"
970 PRINT RF$; TAB( Y);"= ";RF(I);" DAYS"
980 PRINT RG$; TAB( Y);"= ";RG(I);" TIMES"
990 PRINT RH$; TAB( Y);"= ";RH(I);" TIMES"
1000 PRINT
1010 PRINT "PROFITABILITY RATIOS"
1020 PRINT "--------------------"
1030 PRINT RI$; TAB( Y);"= ";RI(I);"%"
1040 PRINT RJ$; TAB( Y);"= ";RJ(I);"%"
1050 PRINT
1060 PRINT : INPUT "CONTINUE? ";C$
1070 RETURN
1080 REM         RATIO NAMES -- STRING INITIALIZATION
1090 RA$ = "- GENERAL"
1100 RB$ = "- IMMEDIATE"
1110 RC$ = "- DEBTS TO ASSETS"
1120 RD$ = "- COVERAGE OF COSTS"
```

```
1130 RE$ = "- INVENTORY TURNOVER"
1140 RF$ = "- AV. COLLECTION TIME"
1150 RG$ = "- FIXED ASSET TURNOVER"
1160 RH$ = "- TOTL ASSET TURNVR"
1170 RI$ = "- PROFIT MARGIN"
1180 RJ$ = "- R.O.I."
1190 R1$ = "LIQUIDITY RATIOS"
1200 R2$ = "LEVERAGE RATIOS"
1210 R3$ = "MANGMT RATIOS"
1220 R4$ = "PROFITABILITY RATIOS"
1230  RETURN
1240  REM       GRAPHICS SUBROUTINE
1250  IF N = 1 GOTO 1570: PRINT : PRINT : PRINT
1260  PRINT : PRINT : PRINT
1270  PRINT "GRAPHIC ANALYSIS OF RATIOS"
1280  PRINT "--------------------------"
1290  PRINT R1$; TAB( Y);"TYPE <1>": PRINT R2$; TAB( Y);"TYPE <2>"
1300  PRINT R3$; TAB( Y);"TYPE <3>": PRINT R4$; TAB( Y);"TYPE <4>"
1310  PRINT "NO GRAPHICS"; TAB( Y);"TYPE <5> ";
1320  INPUT C9: PRINT : PRINT : ON C9 GOTO 1330,1380,1430,1520,1570
1330  PRINT R1$;"  ";RA$:F$ = " TIMES"
1340  FOR I = 1 TO N:W(I) = RA(I): NEXT I: GOSUB 1580
1350  PRINT R1$;"  ";RB$
1360  FOR I = 1 TO N:W(I) = RB(I): NEXT I: GOSUB 1580
1370  GOTO 1260
1380  PRINT R2$;"  ";RC$:F$ = "%"
1390  FOR I = 1 TO N:W(I) = RC(I): NEXT I: GOSUB 1580
1400  PRINT R2$;"  ";RD$:F$ = " TIMES"
1410  FOR I = 1 TO N:W(I) = RD(I): NEXT I: GOSUB 1580
1420  GOTO 1260
1430  PRINT R3$;"  ";RE$
1440  FOR I = 1 TO N:W(I) = RE(I): NEXT I: GOSUB 1580
1450  PRINT R3$;"  ";RF$:F$ = " DAYS"
1460  FOR I = 1 TO N:W(I) = RF(I): NEXT I: GOSUB 1580
1470  PRINT R3$;"  ";RG$:F$ = " TIMES"
1480  FOR I = 1 TO N:W(I) = RG(I): NEXT I: GOSUB 1580
1490  PRINT R3$;"  ";RH$
1500  FOR I = 1 TO N:W(I) = RH(I): NEXT I: GOSUB 1580
1510  GOTO 1260
1520  PRINT R4$;"  ";RI$:F$ = "%"
1530  FOR I = 1 TO N:W(I) = RI(I): NEXT I: GOSUB 1580
1540  PRINT R4$;"  ";RJ$
1550  FOR I = 1 TO N:W(I) = RJ(I): NEXT I: GOSUB 1580
1560  GOTO 1260
1570  RETURN
1580  REM        GRAPHICS OUTPUT SUBROUTINE
1590 C = 0:MI = W(1):MAX = W(1)
1600  FOR I = 1 TO N:C = C + W(I)
1610  IF W(I) < MI THEN MI = W(I)
1620  IF W(I) > MAX THEN MAX = W(I)
1630  NEXT I
1640 AV =  INT (100 * (C / N + .5)) / 100:B = MAX + 10:A = MI - 10
1650  PRINT "YEAR": PRINT "    I"
1660  FOR I = 1 TO N
1670  PRINT I; TAB( 4);"I"; TAB( (W(I) - A) * (32 / (B - A)) + 6);"*"
1680  PRINT "    I": NEXT I
1690  PRINT  TAB( 4): FOR X = 1 TO 32: PRINT "-";: NEXT X: PRINT
1700 X = 0: FOR I = A TO B STEP 10
1710  PRINT  TAB( X * 32 * (10 / (B - A)) + 5); INT (I);
1720 X = X + 1: NEXT I
```

```
1730    PRINT F$: PRINT
1740    FOR I = 1 TO N: PRINT  TAB( 5);I;"= ";W(I);"; ";: NEXT I: PRINT
1750    PRINT  TAB( 5);"HIGH=";MAX;" ";"LOW=";MI;" ";"AVERAGE=";AV
1760    PRINT : PRINT : INPUT "CONTINUE? ";C$
1770    REM
1780    FOR T = 1 TO 15: PRINT : NEXT T
1790    RETURN
```

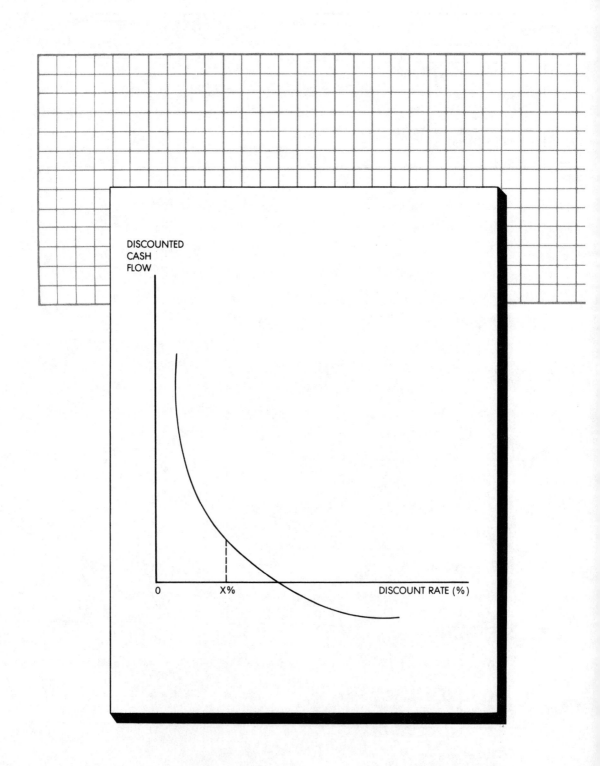

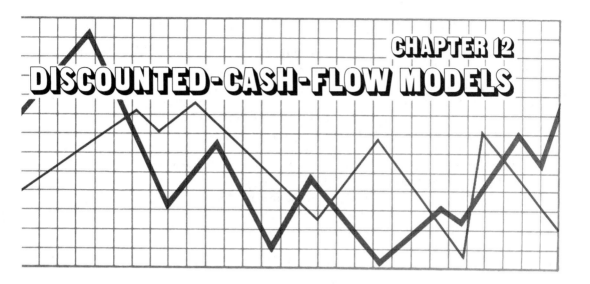

CHAPTER 12
DISCOUNTED-CASH-FLOW MODELS

THE METHOD

This chapter presents two widely used tools for capital-budgeting decisions: the net present value, and internal rate of return. These are variations of what is often called the discounted-cash-flow model, which is used to evaluate a project, while recognizing that a dollar received today is preferable to a dollar received at some future date.

The *net present value* can be defined as the difference between the total discounted gains and the total discounted expenses (including initial cost outlay) of a project during the entire period under analysis. An investment project is financially desirable if the discounted cash-flow is positive. The best choice among several investment options is the one that has the largest discounted cash flow, i.e., the greatest present value.

The hardest part of this technique is determining a *suitable* discount rate. For a point of reference, we can find the discount rate under which the net discounted cash flow will be zero. This value is called the *internal rate of return.* Using this rate, the net discounted gains of the project will be equal to the net discounted expenses.

As an investment criterion, the internal rate of return is compared to a predetermined rate called the *rate of acceptance* or *rate of rejection.* This rate is based on interest expenses on financing for the business.

Normally these two techniques lead to the same end result—acceptance or rejection of an investment project. However, under certain circumstances the two techniques can give different answers since each method assumes a different rate of return on investment for the project. Which method produces better results? The real answer is found in the choice of an adequate rate of return for intermediate reinvested cash flow gains. The ideal solution might be to choose a different rate of return for each investment period to calculate the total present value.

Many studies agree that the net present value method is theoretically superior. The desired rate of return—which must be greater than, or at least equal to financing expenses—is a valid approximation of the rate of return on investment. We can also deduce from this principle of acceptance that among several investment options the one with the high internal rate of return will be the one to take.

THE PROGRAM

This program calculates both the net present value and the internal rate of return of an investment project. The net present value is increased by the discounted residual value (if any) of machinery purchased as part of the investment, and decreased by the original cost of the investment.

It is often useful to calculate a *profitability index.* This percentage gives the relationship between the total discounted gains (including residual value) and the total discounted expenses. An option is viable when its profitability index is greater than or equal to 100%.

Lines 60 to 390 of this program collect, rearrange, and print the data. Note that the instructions **GOSUB** 850 and **GOSUB** 870 simply print the frames and headings of the tables.

The **FOR** loop in lines 430 to 510 computes the present value of the revenue, expense, and profits, respectively, for each period of the project. This loop also accumulates the total values of these three categories for the entire project. Since the residual value is realized for the period *following* the life of the project, its present value is calculated based on period V + 1 (line 530).

Lines 670 to 780 use an iterative technique to compute the internal rate of return (T0). Looping is terminated when the net discounted cash flow equals zero. Via the test in line 740, control jumps out of the loop when the condition:

$$X <= 0$$

is met.

The validity of this model rests on the choice of the discount rate, which is often approximate and subjective. To reduce the risk of a bad estimate, sensitivity analysis is often called for. Such analysis is proposed in lines 810 to 830.

APPLICATION EXAMPLE

The Problem

Jack Tompson is the owner and manager of a small car rental firm. To answer the needs of some of his customers, he is considering the possibility of renting campers. Considering the relatively high cost of campers and his own inexperience with camper rentals, Tompson intends to start with a single camper. He wants to estimate the potential profits of this new operation.

The Data

Information from his supplier and his customers has helped Tompson establish the following forecast:

Year	Income	Expenses
1	$5000	$ 100
2	5500	1000
3	5500	1200
4	5000	1500
5	5000	1500

Purchase price of a camper = $18000
Residual value of the camper in 5 years = $8000

Since Tompson intends to finance the purchase partly on his own, and partly through loans, he has estimated the discount rate in terms of both the cost of the loan, and the opportunity costs implied in the use of his own funds. He estimates this rate to be about 12%.

The Results

The output of the program indicates a net present value of $1286.38. A sensitivity analysis, with discount rates of 10% and 14% respectively, confirm the profitability of the project.

The Output

```
 NET PRESENT VALUE AND
INTERNAL RATE OF RETURN
-----------------------

INITIAL COST OF THE INVESTMENT? 18000

ESTIMATED DURATION OF PROJECT?   5

PERIODIC INCOME FROM PROJECT:
--PERIOD #1    ?5000
--PERIOD #2    ?5500
--PERIOD #3    ?5500
--PERIOD #4    ?5000
--PERIOD #5    ?5000

EXPENSES FORECAST:
--PERIOD #1    ?100
--PERIOD #2    ?1000
--PERIOD #3    ?1200
--PERIOD #4    ?1500
--PERIOD #5    ?1500

RESIDUAL VALUE OF THE INVESTMENT? 8000

RATE OF RETURN ON INVESTMENT? (%) 12

FORECASTS:
-----------------------------------------
PERIOD  EXPECTED  ESTIMATED  EXPECTED
        REVENUES  EXPENSES   PROFITS
-----------------------------------------
   1      5000      100        4900
   2      5500      1000       4500
   3      5500      1200       4300
   4      5000      1500       3500
   5      5000      1500       3500
-----------------------------------------

CONTINUE? Y

PRESENT VALUE:
-----------------------------------------
PERIOD  EXPECTED   ESTIMATED   EXPECTED
        REVENUES   EXPENSES    PROFITS
        (PRES VAL)(PRES VAL)  (PRES VAL)
-----------------------------------------
   1     4464.29    89.29       4375
   2     4384.57    797.19      3587.37
   3     3914.79    854.14      3060.66
   4     3177.59    953.28      2224.31
   5     2837.13    851.14      1985.99
-----------------------------------------
PRESENT VALUE OF RESIDUAL =    4053.05
-----------------------------------------

CONTINUE? Y
```

```
RESULTS OF THE ANALYSIS:
-------------------------------------
NET PRESENT VALUE OF CASH-FLOW
(INCLUDING RESIDUAL VALUE) =  1286.38
-------------------------------------
PROFITABILITY INDEX =         105.97%
-------------------------------------
INTERNAL RATE OF RETURN =     14.4%
-------------------------------------


PERFORM SENSITIVITY ANALYSIS BY
MODIFYING THE RATE OF RETURN? (Y/N) N
```

The Program Listing

```
1   REM        NET PRESENT VALUE
2   REM        BUI        5/81
3   REM
4   REM        VARIABLES
5   REM        B          TOTAL DISCOUNTED PROFITS
6   REM        B(I)       PROFIT FOR PERIOD I
7   REM        B1(I)      DISCOUNTED PROFIT FOR PERIOD I
8   REM        C          INITIAL COST OF PROJECT
9   REM        D(I)       EXPENSES FOR PERIOD I
10  REM        DD         TOTAL DISCOUNTED EXPENSES
11  REM        D1(I)      DISCOUNTED EXPENSES FOR PERIOD I
12  REM        R(I)       REVENUES FOR PERIOD I
13  REM        R0         RESIDUAL VALUE OF PROJECT
14  REM        R1(I)      DISCOUNTED REVENUES FOR PERIOD I
15  REM        T          DISCOUNT RATE
16  REM        V          ESTIMATED DURATION OF PROJECT
17  REM        VR         DISCOUNTED RESIDUAL VALUE
18  REM
19  DEF   FN A(X) =   INT (100 * X + .5) / 100
20  PRINT : PRINT
30  PRINT " NET PRESENT VALUE AND"
40  PRINT "INTERNAL RATE OF RETURN"
45  PRINT "-----------------------"
50  PRINT : PRINT
60  INPUT "INITIAL COST OF THE INVESTMENT? ";C
70  PRINT
80  INPUT "ESTIMATED DURATION OF PROJECT?   ";V
90  DIM R(V),D(V),B(V),R1(V),D1(V),B1(V)
100  PRINT
110  PRINT "PERIODIC INCOME FROM PROJECT:"
120  FOR I = 1 TO V
130  PRINT "--PERIOD #";I; TAB( 15);
140  INPUT R(I)
150  NEXT I: PRINT
160  PRINT "EXPENSES FORECAST:"
170  FOR I = 1 TO V
180  PRINT "--PERIOD #";I; TAB( 15);
190  INPUT D(I)
```

```
200    NEXT I: PRINT
210    INPUT "RESIDUAL VALUE OF THE INVESTMENT? ";RO
220    PRINT
230    INPUT "RATE OF RETURN ON INVESTMENT? (%) ";T
240    REM        PRINT OUTPUT
250    PRINT : PRINT
260    PRINT "FORECASTS:"
270    GOSUB 850
280    GOSUB 870
290    GOSUB 850
300    FOR I = 1 TO V
310    B(I) = R(I) - D(I)
320    PRINT  TAB( 3);I; TAB( 10);R(I); TAB( 20);D(I); TAB( 31);B(I)
330    NEXT I
340    GOSUB 850
345    INPUT "CONTINUE? ";C$
350    PRINT : PRINT : PRINT
360    REM        PRESENT VALUE
370    PRINT "PRESENT VALUE: "
380    GOSUB 850
390    GOSUB 870
395    P$ = "(PRES VAL)"
400    PRINT  TAB( 9);P$; TAB( 19);P$; TAB( 30);P$
410    GOSUB 850
420    B = 0:RR = 0:DD = 0
430    FOR I = 1 TO V
440    R1(I) = R(I) * (1 + T / 100) ^ ( - I)
450    D1(I) = D(I) * (1 + T / 100) ^ ( - I)
460    B1(I) = R1(I) - D1(I)
470    B = B + B1(I)
480    RR = RR + R1(I)
490    DD = DD + D1(I)
500    PRINT  TAB( 3); FN A(I); TAB( 10); FN A(R1(I));
505    PRINT  TAB( 20); FN A(D1(I)); TAB( 31); FN A(B1(I))
510    NEXT I
520    GOSUB 850
530    VR = RO * (1 + T / 100) ^ ( - V - 1)
540    PRINT "PRESENT VALUE OF RESIDUAL = ";
550    PRINT  TAB( 31); FN A(VR)
560    GOSUB 850
565    PRINT : INPUT "CONTINUE? ";C$
570    REM        PRINT OUTPUT
580    PRINT : PRINT
590    PRINT "RESULTS OF THE ANALYSIS:"
600    GOSUB 850
610    PRINT "NET PRESENT VALUE OF CASH-FLOW"
620    PRINT "(INCLUDING RESIDUAL VALUE)";
630    PRINT " = "; TAB( 31); FN A(B + VR - C)
640    GOSUB 850
650    PRINT "PROFITABILITY INDEX = ";
660    PRINT  TAB( 31); INT (10000 * ((RR + VR) / (DD + C)) + .5) / 100;"%"
670    REM        CALCULATE INTERNAL RATE OF RETURN
680    FOR TO = 0 TO 100 STEP 0.1
690    X = 0
700    FOR I = 1 TO V
710    X = X + B(I) * (1 + TO / 100) ^ ( - I)
720    NEXT I
730    X = X + RO * (1 + TO / 100) ^ ( - V - 1) - C
740    IF X < = 0 THEN 760
750    NEXT TO
```

```
760   GOSUB 850
770   PRINT "INTERNAL RATE OF RETURN = ";
780   PRINT  TAB( 31); FN A(T0);"%"
790   GOSUB 850
800   PRINT : PRINT
810   PRINT "PERFORM SENSITIVITY ANALYSIS BY "
820   INPUT "MODIFYING THE RATE OF RETURN? (Y/N) ";C$
830   IF  LEFT$ (C$,1) <  > "N" THEN 220
840   END
850   PRINT "------------------------------------"
860   RETURN
870   PRINT "PERIOD  EXPECTED  ESTIMATED  EXPECTED"
880   PRINT "        REVENUES  EXPENSES   PROFITS "
890   RETURN
```

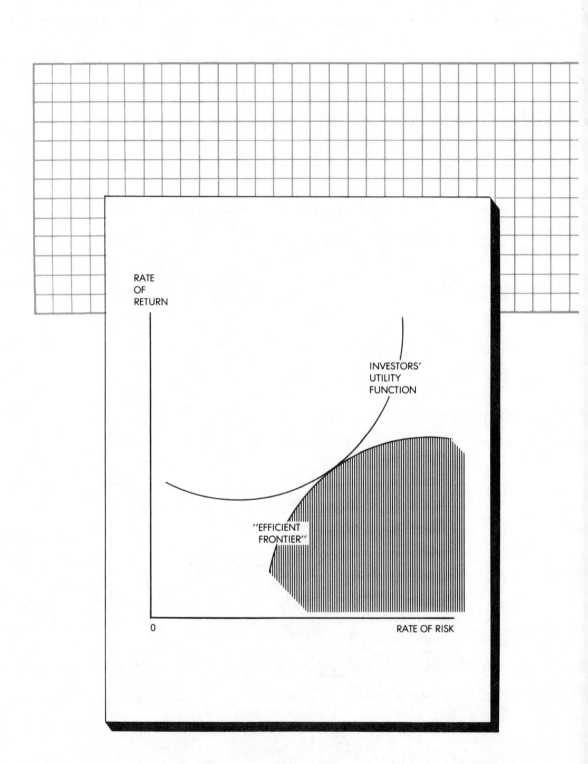

RATE
OF
RETURN

INVESTORS'
UTILITY
FUNCTION

"EFFICIENT
FRONTIER"

0   RATE OF RISK

CHAPTER 13
PORTFOLIO MANAGEMENT

THE METHOD

This chapter analyzes investment portfolio management. The program develops the well-known model of H. Markowitz, whose technique is based on selection of a diversified portfolio.

If rate of return were the only factor in a stock portfolio, it would be easy to choose investments for maximum income. However, the greater the potential return on an investment, the greater tends to be the risk. A wise investor will therefore divide up the risk in a group of good investments, or a *diversified portfolio*. In this context, the main task of portfolio management is to reach a reasonable equilibrium between expected gain and the risk associated with this gain.

The total gain on a stock investment during a given period is equal to the dividends received plus the increase in value of the stock. Thus the rate of return can be expressed as:

$$R_{it} = \frac{D_{it} + (V_{it} - V_{i(t-1)})}{V_{i(t-1)}}$$

where:

> R_{it} = Rate of return of stock i during period t.
> D_{it} = Dividends received.
> V_{it} = Value of stock i at the end of period t.
> $V_{i(t-1)}$ = Value of stock i at the end of period $(t-1)$.

If it is assumed a *priori* that this rate will be maintained in the future, then the expected return on investment can be determined from the average rates of return of past periods. This can be calculated as a simple arithmetic mean.

The notion of risk, or uncertainty, is based on the fact that expected returns are not always realized. The risk is thus an indication of the possible deviation from the rate of return. To measure this uncertainty, we use an indicator that is well known to statisticians: the *variance*, (σ^2), or the *standard deviation* (σ). The variance is calculated from the following formula:

$$\sigma_i^2 = \frac{1}{n} \sum_{t=1}^{n} (R_{it} - \bar{R}_i)^2$$

where:

> σ_i^2 = Variance of stock i during the entire period of analysis.
> R_{it} = Rate of return of stock i during period t.
> R_i = Average rate of return of stock i during the entire period of analysis.

Once the concepts of rate of return and risk have been defined, they can be applied at the portfolio level. Given a portfolio composed of n stocks, the average rate of return (R_p), and the risk of the portfolio (σ_p^2) are defined as follows:

$$\bar{R}_p = \sum_{i=1}^{n} \bar{R}_i X_i$$

$$\sigma_p^2 = \sum_{i=1}^{n} \sigma_i^2 X_i^2$$

where:

> X_i = The amount invested in stock i.

Note that the risk of the portfolio is less than the sum of the risks of the stocks that constitute it. This is because we assume in this formulation that each stock fluctuates completely *independently* of the others. Thus, to reduce the total risk of a portfolio the investor should retain stocks that are only slightly interdependent.

To quantify this interdependence, we refer to the statistical concept of *covariance;* the covariance can be included in the definition of portfolio risk. When the covariances of the stocks in a portfolio range from positive to negative values, we can expect that the stock fluctuations will tend to balance each other out, contributing to a reduction in the risk of the total portfolio.

The Program

This is a quadratic optimization program based on Markowitz's well-known model of the *mean-variance.* Given the individual rates of return and risk defined above, the program supplies the investor with a series of "efficient" portfolio distributions, either minimizing the risk for a given expected return or maximizing the return for a given risk. This interactive program thus allows the investor to explore the results of diversification and in particular to discover means of reducing investment risk.

Two important comments apply to the use of this program:

1. In its present form, the program supposes perfect independence in the behavior of the stocks that make up the portfolio; that is, the covariances are zero. This simplification results in an underestimate of the risk. The covariances could be introduced at the beginning in a minor revision of the program.

2. Since the rates of return and risk are often calculated based on relatively long observation periods (one month, six months, one year, depending on the distribution of dividends), use of the mean-variance model is recommended for medium-term portfolio management (semi-annual, annual). Unless economic or political factors upset the stock exchange dramatically, too frequent modifications of small or medium portfolios may lead to losses in terms of time and the costs of transactions.

This program is an excellent exercise in matrix operations. The objective is to determine the array X(I) (where I = 1 to N) that represents the optimal distribution (in %) of the securities. (The sum of the elements of X will thus be equal to 1.)

The array X(I) is defined by the following formula:

$$X = P^{-1} B' (BP^{-1}B')^{-1}T$$

where:

P^{-1} represents the *inverse* of matrix P, and
B' represents the *transpose* of matrix B

(See the variable list of the program for the definition of each element of this equation.)

Lines 60 to 350 form the input routine. Since the program assumes a perfect independence between the variations of the securities (i.e., co-variances of zero), all of the elements of matrix P are zero except for the diagonal. (The diagonal represents the variances.) The model can thus be improved by replacing lines 250 to 270 with appropriate **INPUT** instructions for the covariances. Alternatively, the second program of Appendix A can be incorporated into this program for input of raw data.

Lines 370 to 730, and the associated subroutines, develop the matrix equation shown above (Equation 1). Note the following three elements of the program:

1. The matrix inversion subroutine (lines 1030 to 1200) uses a short and rapid algorithm for the inversion of a nonsingular square matrix. If the program stops at line 1090, the matrix inversion is not possible.

2. The subroutine that identifies the "efficient frontier" (lines 1210 to 1560) finds the extreme return-risk pairs that define the range of profitability of the portfolio. The variable M3 represents the expected rate of return associated with a minimum risk; M4, on the other hand, is the maximum rate of return, associated with the highest reasonable risk. The loop in lines 1470 to 1540 calculates ten return-risk pairs that fall between M3 and M4. To see more steps between the minimum and the maximum levels of the efficient frontier, replace the 10 in line 1470 with a larger number.

3. The array element T(2), representing the expected rate of return, is input by the user. The **GOTO** loop from line 980 up to line 640 allows the user to investigate "optimal composition" tables for several different rates of return in an analysis of risk aversion.

Lines 750 to 960 produce these tables, including a summary of the portfolio's expected performance (lines 800 to 860). Note that the risk is expressed in terms of the standard deviation, i.e., the square root of the variance. Finally, lines 880 to 960 display the distribution of the securities in the portfolio, both in percents and dollars.

APPLICATION EXAMPLE

The Problem

Jackson's Moving Company is a family business that presently enjoys a particularly healthy financial situation, with considerable cash assets. Barbara Jackson, the owner and director of the business, wants to invest some of the short-term assets in stocks and bonds, to the amount of $200,000.

The Data

Keeping in mind the little time she has available for portfolio analysis, Jackson selects a portfolio of twelve securities from a list supplied by her bank—three banks, three insurance companies, four industrial stocks, and two commercial stocks. Jackson wants to know the expected returns and risks of her portfolio, and is exploring the best way to divide up the purchase of titles. The following table presents the average rates of return and the standard deviations of the twelve investments (calculations based on 24 monthly measurements):

Stock	Average Rate of Return	Standard Deviation of Rates of Return in %
1. Bank 1	6.75	1.70
2. Bank 2	7.00	2.05
3. Bank 3	7.20	2.10
4. Insurance 1	6.60	1.50
5. Insurance 2	7.10	2.30
6. Insurance 3	8.12	3.12
7. Industry 1	11.87	5.25
8. Industry 2	10.76	4.75
9. Industry 3	13.50	7.05
10. Industry 4	11.50	6.60
11. Commerce 1	9.75	4.75
12. Commerce 2	8.50	3.50

The Results

See the output of the example. The program proposes an efficient range of portfolio combinations, where the performance varies from 7.11% return (with a .76% risk) to 9.39% return (1.33% risk). Depending on the investor, a low-profit, low-risk or a high-profit, high-risk portfolio can be chosen.

Based on a 7.5% rate of return (i.e., $15,000 on the original $200,000), Jackson's portfolio will be distributed according to the first table entitled "Optimal Composition of the Portfolio." Notice that the first five titles take up more than 75% of the portfolio.

The second "Optimal Composition" table shows a new division of the investments for a rate of return of 10%. Note that 10% goes beyond the suggested "efficient" range initially calculated by the program; thus, one of the values turns up negative (Insurance 1 = −3.94). This title should be removed from the portfolio for a rate of return of 10% or more.

Finally, the third table shows the division for a smaller investment ($100,000) with an expected rate of return of 9.6%.

The Output

```
FINANCIAL ASSET PORTFOLIO MANAGEMENT
------------------------------------


NUMBER OF SECURITIES? 12


NAME:
- OF SECURITY 1      ?BANK1
- OF SECURITY 2      ?BANK2
- OF SECURITY 3      ?BANK3
- OF SECURITY 4      ?INSURANCE1
- OF SECURITY 5      ?INSURANCE2
- OF SECURITY 6      ?INSURANCE3
- OF SECURITY 7      ?INDUSTRY1
- OF SECURITY 8      ?INDUSTRY2
- OF SECURITY 9      ?INDUSTRY3
- OF SECURITY 10     ?INDUSTRY4
- OF SECURITY 11     ?COMMERCE1
- OF SECURITY 12     ?COMMERCE2




AVERAGE RATE OF RETURN IN % :
- OF BANK1 SECURITY          ?6.75
- OF BANK2 SECURITY          ?7
- OF BANK3 SECURITY          ?7.2
- OF INSURANCE1 SECURITY     ?6.6
- OF INSURANCE2 SECURITY     ?7.1
- OF INSURANCE3 SECURITY     ?8.12
- OF INDUSTRY1 SECURITY      ?11.87
- OF INDUSTRY2 SECURITY      ?10.76
- OF INDUSTRY3 SECURITY      ?13.50
- OF INDUSTRY4 SECURITY      ?11.50
- OF COMMERCE1 SECURITY      ?9.75
- OF COMMERCE2 SECURITY      ?8.5




RATE OF RISK (STANDARD DEVIATION) IN %:
- OF BANK1 SECURITY          ?1.70
- OF BANK2 SECURITY          ?2.05
- OF BANK3 SECURITY          ?2.10
- OF INSURANCE1 SECURITY     ?1.50
- OF INSURANCE2 SECURITY     ?2.30
- OF INSURANCE3 SECURITY     ?3.12
- OF INDUSTRY1 SECURITY      ?5.25
- OF INDUSTRY2 SECURITY      ?4.75
- OF INDUSTRY3 SECURITY      ?7.05
- OF INDUSTRY4 SECURITY      ?6.60
- OF COMMERCE1 SECURITY      ?4.75
- OF COMMERCE2 SECURITY      ?3.50
```

```
EFFICIENT FRONTIER OF PORTFOLIO
-------------------------------
    EXPECTED        ASSOCIATED
    RETURN            RISK
     (%)              (%)
   ---------       ----------
     7.11             .76
     7.37             .75
     7.62             .76
     7.87             .79
     8.13             .84
     8.38             .92
     8.63            1.01
     8.88            1.11
     9.14            1.21
     9.39            1.33
-------------------------------

CHOOSE AN EXPECTED RATE OF RETURN?(Y/N)Y

EXPECTED RATE OF RETURN
ON THE PORTFOLIO (IN %) ?7.5

TOTAL AMOUNT OF INVESTMENT ($)? 200000


OPTIMAL COMPOSITION OF THE PORTFOLIO
----------------------------------------
    NUMBER OF SECURITIES    : 12
    TOTAL INVESTMENT        : $200000
    EXPECTED RETURN         : $15000
    ASSOCIATED RISK         : $1495.46


----------------------------------------
NAME OF SECURITY        % OF     AMOUNT IN $
                      PORTFOLIO
----------------      ---------  -----------
1   BANK1               18.63     37256.99
2   BANK2               12.98     25950.07
3   BANK3               12.49     24979.86
4   INSURANCE1          23.74     47485.88
5   INSURANCE2          10.36     20719.88
6   INSURANCE3           5.92     11839.32
7   INDUSTRY1            2.47      4933.73
8   INDUSTRY2            2.88      5755.02
9   INDUSTRY3            1.46      2917.35
10  INDUSTRY4            1.54      3074.83
11  COMMERCE1            2.75      5507.48
12  COMMERCE2            4.79      9579.6
----------------------------------------

CHOOSE AN EXPECTED RATE OF RETURN?(Y/N)Y

EXPECTED RATE OF RETURN
ON THE PORTFOLIO (IN %) ?10


TOTAL AMOUNT OF INVESTMENT ($)? 200000
```

```
OPTIMAL COMPOSITION OF THE PORTFOLIO
------------------------------------------
    NUMBER OF SECURITIES    : 12
    TOTAL INVESTMENT        : $200000
    EXPECTED RETURN         : $20000
    ASSOCIATED RISK         : $3237.08

------------------------------------------
NAME OF SECURITY      % OF      AMOUNT IN $
                      PORTFOLIO
----------------      ---------  -----------
1  BANK1                1.07       2130.71
2  BANK2                5.47      10942.73
3  BANK3                8.83      17653.07
4  INSURANCE1          -3.94      -7884.3
5  INSURANCE2           5.85      11704.81
6  INSURANCE3          11.53      23054.42
7  INDUSTRY1           14.91      29817.93
8  INDUSTRY2           14.29      28587.95
9  INDUSTRY3           10.88      21760.32
10 INDUSTRY4            8.76      17514
11 COMMERCE1           10.73      21456.24
12 COMMERCE2           11.63      23262.13
------------------------------------------

CHOOSE AN EXPECTED RATE OF RETURN?(Y/N)Y

EXPECTED RATE OF RETURN
ON THE PORTFOLIO (IN %) ?9.6

TOTAL AMOUNT OF INVESTMENT ($)? 100000

OPTIMAL COMPOSITION OF THE PORTFOLIO
------------------------------------------
    NUMBER OF SECURITIES    : 12
    TOTAL INVESTMENT        : $100000
    EXPECTED RETURN         : $9600
    ASSOCIATED RISK         : $1425.35
------------------------------------------
NAME OF SECURITY      % OF      AMOUNT IN $
                      PORTFOLIO
----------------      ---------  -----------
1  BANK1                3.88       3875.46
2  BANK2                6.67       6671.95
3  BANK3                9.41       9412.68
4  INSURANCE1            .49        487.46
5  INSURANCE2           6.57       6573.61
6  INSURANCE3          10.63      10630
7  INDUSTRY1           12.92      12918.23
8  INDUSTRY2           12.47      12467.34
9  INDUSTRY3            9.37       9372.72
10 INDUSTRY4            7.6        7601.87
11 COMMERCE1            9.45       9452.22
12 COMMERCE2           10.54      10536.46
------------------------------------------

CHOOSE AN EXPECTED RATE OF RETURN?(Y/N)N

ANOTHER ANALYSIS? N
```

The Program Listing

```
1   REM         PORTFOLIO MANAGEMENT PROGRAM
2   REM         THE MEAN-VARIANCE MODEL
3   REM         BUI         1981
4   REM
5   REM         VARIABLES
6   REM         A$(I)        ARRAY OF STRINGS
7   REM                      TO IDENTIFY SECURITIES
8   REM         B(2,I)       RATE OF RETURN OF
9   REM                      SECURITY I
10  REM         M3           MINIMUM RATE OF RETURN
11  REM                      WITH A MINIMUM RISK
12  REM         M4           HIGHEST RATE OF RETURN
13  REM                      WITH REASONABLE RISK
14  REM         N            NUMBER OF SECURITIES
15  REM         P(I,J)       VARIANCE-COVARIANCE MATRIX
16  REM         T(K)         ARRAY WITH TWO ELEMENTS:
17  REM                      T(1) = 1 (I.E., 100% OF PORTFOLIO)
18  REM                      T(2) = DESIRED RATE OF RETURN
19  REM                           FROM PORTFOLIO
20  REM         T3           TOTAL AMOUNT OF INVESTMENT
21  REM         X(I)         PROPORTION (% OF TOTAL
22  REM                      PORTFOLIO) OF SECURITY I
23  REM
24  PRINT : PRINT : PRINT
30  PRINT "FINANCIAL ASSET PORTFOLIO MANAGEMENT"
40  PRINT "-----------------------------------"
50  PRINT : PRINT : PRINT
60  INPUT "NUMBER OF SECURITIES? ";N
70  PRINT
80  DIM A$(N),B(2,N),B1(N,2),P(N,N),P1(N,N)
90  DIM T(2),C(N,2),C1(N,2),X(N),M1(N),M2(N)
100 N1 = N
110  PRINT "NAME:"
120  FOR I = 1 TO N
130  PRINT "- OF SECURITY ";I; TAB( 20);
140  INPUT A$(I)
150  NEXT I
160  PRINT : PRINT
170  PRINT "AVERAGE RATE OF RETURN IN % :"
180  FOR I = 1 TO N
190 B(1,I) = 1:B1(I,1) = 1
200  PRINT "- OF ";A$(I);" SECURITY"; TAB( 30);
210  INPUT B(2,I)
220 B(2,I) = B(2,I) / 100:B1(I,2) = B(2,I)
230  NEXT I
240  REM
250  FOR I = 1 TO N: FOR J = 1 TO N
260 P(I,J) = 0
270  NEXT J,I
280  PRINT : PRINT
290  PRINT "RATE OF RISK (STANDARD DEVIATION) IN %:"
300  FOR I = 1 TO N
310  PRINT "- OF ";A$(I);" SECURITY"; TAB( 30);
320  INPUT P(I,I)
330 P(I,I) = (P(I,I) / 100) ^ 2
340 P1(I,I) = P(I,I)
350  NEXT I
360  PRINT
370 T(1) = 1
```

```
380  REM        QUADRATIC OPTIMIZATION
390  GOSUB 1030
400  FOR I = 1 TO N
410   FOR K = 1 TO 2
420  C(I,K) = 0
430   FOR J = 1 TO N
440  C(I,K) = C(I,K) + P(I,J) * B1(J,K)
450  C1(I,K) = C(I,K)
460  NEXT J,K,I
470   FOR I = 1 TO 2
480   FOR K = 1 TO 2
490  P(I,K) = 0
500   FOR J = 1 TO N
510  P(I,K) = P(I,K) + B(I,J) * C1(J,K)
520  NEXT. J,K,I
530  N = 2
540   GOSUB 1030
550  N = N1
560   FOR I = 1 TO N
570   FOR K = 1 TO 2
580  C(I,K) = 0
590   FOR J = 1 TO 2
600  C(I,K) = C(I,K) + C1(I,J) * P(J,K)
610  NEXT J,K,I
620   GOSUB 1210
630  PRINT : PRINT
640  INPUT "CHOOSE AN EXPECTED RATE OF RETURN?(Y/N)";C$
650  IF  LEFT$ (C$,1) = "N" THEN 990
660  PRINT
670  PRINT "EXPECTED RATE OF RETURN "
675  INPUT "ON THE PORTFOLIO (IN %) ?";T(2)
680  PRINT :T(2) = T(2) / 100
690   FOR I = 1 TO N
700  X(I) = 0
710   FOR J = 1 TO 2
720  X(I) = X(I) + C(I,J) * T(J)
730  NEXT J,I
740  PRINT
750  INPUT "TOTAL AMOUNT OF INVESTMENT ($)? ";T3
760  REM        PRINT RESULTS
765  DEF  FN R(X) =  INT (100 * X + .5) / 100
770  PRINT : PRINT : PRINT
780  PRINT "OPTIMAL COMPOSITION OF THE PORTFOLIO"
790  PRINT "-------------------------------------"
800  PRINT "   NUMBER OF SECURITIES    : ";N
810  PRINT "   TOTAL INVESTMENT        : $";T3
820  PRINT "   EXPECTED RETURN         : $"; FN R(T(2) * T3)
830  FOR I = 1 TO N
840  VR = VR + P1(I,I) * ((C(I,1) * T(1) + C(I,2) * T(2)) ^ 2)
850  NEXT I
860  PRINT "   ASSOCIATED RISK         : $" FN R(( SQR (VR)) * T3)
870  PRINT
880  PRINT "-------------------------------------"
890  PRINT "NAME OF SECURITY    % OF     AMOUNT IN $"
900  PRINT "               PORTFOLIO"
910  PRINT "---------------  ---------  -----------"
920  FOR I = 1 TO N
930  PRINT I; TAB( 4);A$(I); TAB( 21); INT (10000 * X(I) + .5) / 100;
940  PRINT  TAB( 31); FN R(X(I) * T3)
950  NEXT I
960  PRINT "-------------------------------------"
970 VR = 0: PRINT : PRINT
```

```
 980   GOTO 640
 990   PRINT
1000    INPUT "ANOTHER ANALYSIS? ";C$
1010    IF  LEFT$ (C$,1) = "Y" THEN 50
1020   GOTO 9999
1030   REM        MATRIX INVERSION
1040   K = N
1050    FOR L = 1 TO K
1060   X = P(L,L)
1070   P(L,L) = 1
1080    FOR J = 1 TO K
1090   P(L,J) = P(L,J) / X
1100    NEXT J
1110    FOR I = 1 TO K
1120    IF I = L THEN 1180
1130   X = P(I,L)
1140   P(I,L) = 0
1150    FOR J = 1 TO K
1160   P(I,J) = P(I,J) - X * P(L,J)
1170    NEXT J
1180    NEXT I
1190    NEXT L
1200    RETURN
1210   REM         IDENTIFICATION OF EFFICIENT FRONTIER OF PORTFOLIO
1220   REM         DEFINITION OF INTERVALS
1230    FOR I = 1 TO N
1240   M1(I) = ( - C(I,1) * T(1)) / C(I,2)
1250   M2(I) = (T(1) - C(I,1) * T(1)) / C(I,2)
1260    NEXT I
1270    FOR I = 1 TO N
1280    IF M2(I) >  = M1(I) THEN 1320
1290   M3 = M2(I)
1300   M2(I) = M1(I)
1310   M1(I) = M3
1320    NEXT I
1330   M3 = M1(1)
1340   M4 = M2(1)
1350   REM        CALCULATE MAXIMUM LOWER LIMIT AND
1360   REM        MINIMUM UPPER LIMIT
1370    FOR I = 2 TO N
1380    IF M1(I) > M3 THEN M3 = M1(I)
1390    IF M2(I) < M4 THEN M4 = M2(I)
1400    NEXT I
1410    PRINT : PRINT : PRINT
1420    PRINT "EFFICIENT FRONTIER OF PORTFOLIO"
1430    PRINT "-------------------------------"
1440    PRINT "    EXPECTED      ASSOCIATED    "
1445    PRINT "     RETURN         RISK"
1450    PRINT "      (%)           (%)"
1460    PRINT "    --------      ---------"
1470    FOR J = M3 TO M4 STEP (M4 - M3) / 10
1480    FOR I = 1 TO N
1490   VR = VR + P1(I,I) * ((C(I,1) * T(1) + C(I,2) * J) ^ 2)
1500    NEXT I
1510    PRINT  TAB( 7); INT (10000 * J + .5) / 100;
1520    PRINT  TAB( 21); INT (10000 *  SQR (VR) + .5) / 100
1530   VR = 0
1540    NEXT J
1550    PRINT "-------------------------------"
1560    RETURN
9999    END
```

SECTION V

MULTICRITERIA

DECISION-AID

MODEL

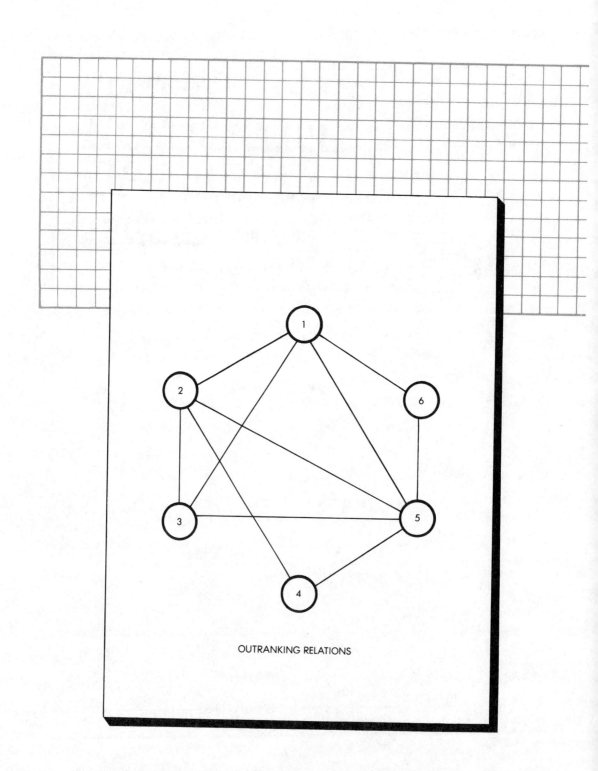

OUTRANKING RELATIONS

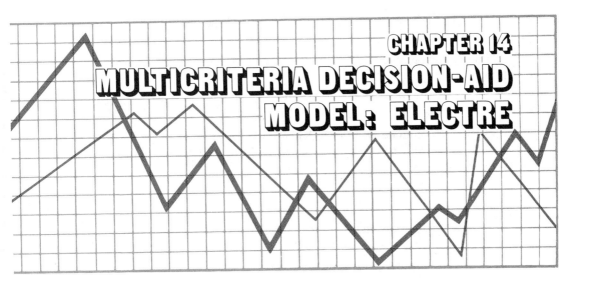

CHAPTER 14
MULTICRITERIA DECISION-AID
MODEL: ELECTRE

THE METHOD

This chapter describes the French-developed multicriteria decision-aid model known as Electre. Two important features distinguish Electre from most other business management decision models:

1. The model allows analysis of *several criteria* at once. These criteria may be either quantifiable (cost, weight, etc.) or non-quantifiable (quality of service, aesthetics, etc.). The criteria may also present complex or contradictory elements ("economicity" of production and pollution, etc.).

2. The model also allows consideration of *subjective evaluation,* which can be very important in decision problems.

Electre is based on paired comparisons of the options taken into consideration. This principle is based on a rule expressed as follows by the 18th century French philosopher, the Marquis de Condorset (1750):

> *When an action A is better than another action B in the majority of decision criteria, and, in addition, there is no criterion by which A is clearly worse than B, we can say without risk that A is better than B, or, in other words, A outranks B.*

Two conditions, implied by this principle, form the basis of the Electre decision algorithm:

1. A condition of *concordance,* which requires that a majority of viewpoints favor A.
2. A condition of *discordance,* which requires that no criterion favor B excessively.

Electre uses the concordance and discordance coefficients to make paired comparisons between different options. The concordance coefficient is expressed as follows:

$$C_{A/B} = \frac{\text{Sum of the weights of the criteria by which } A \text{ outranks } B}{\text{Sum of the weights of all the criteria of the model}}$$

It indicates to what extent one option is better than another. The discordance coefficient is calculated from evaluation scores, not weights:

$$D_{A/B} = \frac{\text{The greatest negative variation (i.e., } B \text{ outranks } A\text{) between the evaluation scores for a single criterion}}{\text{The maximum range between the highest possible score and the lowest possible score}}$$

This coefficient indicates to what extent an option contains discordant elements that might make the option unsatisfactory. Both of these factors vary from 0 to 1. A perfect value for the concordance coefficient is 1; a "fatal" score for the discordance coefficient is 1.

These factors are used in conjunction with concordance and discordance "thresholds," chosen arbitrarily by the user. The concordance threshold, P, varies from 0.5 to 1, and is more severe as it approaches 1;

the discordance threshold, Q, is more severe as it approaches 0. We can summarize the rules of the Electre method in the following way:

If	Then
$C_{A/B} >= P$ and $D_{A/B} <= Q$	A outranks B
$C_{B/A} >= P$ and $D_{B/A} <= Q$	B outranks A
A outranks B, and B outranks A	The options are equivalent
Otherwise	The comparison is characterized by indetermination or incomparability

THE PROGRAM

The object of the Electre model is to add structure to the evaluation process of decision-making. It helps the decision-maker analyze preferences with objectivity and confidence. Adding the feature of sensitivity analysis, Electre is one of the best multicriteria decision-aid approaches when we are faced with choosing one option among several.

The heart of the Electre algorithm is expressed in three subroutines: the concordance matrix (lines 810 to 930), the discordance matrix (lines 940 to 1170), and the outranking matrix (lines 1180 to 1250). The background of these subroutines was described in the first section of this chapter.

The input routine takes up a large part of the program, and is designed for easy use by business managers. Since the program may be used several times to aid in any given decision process, it is useful to incorporate certain recurring data values into the program itself. Thus, without using either file handling features or **READ/DATA** instructions, lines 360 to 400 create a "standard" grade-point matrix with five levels for each criterion (excellent = 5; good = 4; average = 3; fair = 2; weak = 1). Also, line 620 provides the user the option of giving equal weight to all the criteria.

Lines 690 to 790 offer options for sensitivity analysis. The new threshold levels P and Q test the stability of the results, i.e., the outranking relations. A new weighting of the criteria indicates a change of mind on the part of the decision maker.

To make this program readily accessible to all versions of BASIC, the **PRINT USING** instruction has not been used to print the matrices. Lines 1260 to 1680 contain a practical method of printing all three matrices by converting numeric values into strings (using the **STR$** function). This technique also makes it easy to place hyphens (-) in the diagonal position of the matrices, where numeric values would be meaningless.

APPLICATION EXAMPLE

The Problem

M. Castella, president of Castella Enterprises, Inc., is searching for a replacement for his head accountant, who is retiring. Five applicants answered his advertisement placed in the business section of a local newspaper. After studying their resumes, Castella eliminated two of the applicants, whose qualifications were good, but not precisely what he wanted. The remaining three applicants present a difficult choice; none of them stands out from the others as clearly the best choice.

The Data

Definition of options. The options represent all the different actions that are possible. In this case, the three applicants will be referred to as A1, A2, and A3.

Definition of criteria. The criteria are the reference points for the comparison. Castella has decided on the following five criteria: Education, Experience, Adaptability, Sociability, and Health.

Weight of the criteria. Castella places different levels of importance on the five criteria. He divides up these weights (out of a total of 100) as follows:

1. Education   15
2. Experience   15
3. Adaptability   20
4. Sociability   30
5. Health   20

Grading system. Castella intends to give grades to each applicant for each criterion. He has established the following table of points to award for each grade:

	Criteria				
	1	**2**	**3**	**4**	**5**
Excellent	10	10	10	20	15
Good	8	8	8	15	10
Average	5	5	5	10	5
Fair	0	1	1	0	3
Weak	0	0	0	0	1

Evaluation of the applicants. The following are the scores awarded to each applicant for each criterion:

Applicant	Criteria				
	1	**2**	**3**	**4**	**5**
A1	8	8	5	15	10
A2	10	1	8	10	15
A3	5	10	8	20	10

The Results

See the output of the example. Examining the concordance matrix, we see that A3 receives a favorable score over the others (a concordance factor of .85 over A1, and .65 over A2). This relative superiority of A3 is due to the importance that Castella gives the sociability criterion. In addition, none of the discordance factors is strong enough to oppose the choice of A3.

The "outranking matrix" is a binary representation of the one-to-one comparisons of the three candidates; a 1 represents the case where one candidate outranks another; a 0 means that neither candidate is clearly better. In the first comparison matrix we see only one outranking, that of A3 over A1. The choice between A2 and A3 is not clear.

On the other hand, if we lower the concordance threshold (from .8 to .6, as shown in the second ranking matrix), meaning that we are applying a less severe concordance criterion, A3 is obviously the best applicant.

The Output

```
     E L E C T R E    1
     -----------------


  ** MULTICRITERIA DECISION-AID MODEL

** NUMBER OF CANDIDATES? 3
** NAMES OF CANDIDATES?
   (ABBREVIATE IN 3 LETTERS)
?A1
?A2
?A3

** NUMBER OF CRITERIA? 5

  ** EVALUATION TABLE
     ---------- -----
     YOU HAVE TWO OPTIONS:
     - FOR A STANDARD SCALE, TYPE <1>
     - FOR YOUR OWN SCALE,   TYPE <2>
     INDICATE YOUR CHOICE: 2
```

```
** NUMBER OF CLASSES IN THE SCALE? 5


INPUT YOUR EVALUATION TABLE:

5 CRITERIA FOR CLASS 1
?10
?10
?10
?20
?15
5 CRITERIA FOR CLASS 2
?8
?8
?8
?15
?10
5 CRITERIA FOR CLASS 3
?5
?5
?5
?10
?5
5 CRITERIA FOR CLASS 4
?0
?1
?1
?0
?3
5 CRITERIA FOR CLASS 5
?0
?0
?0
?0
?1

** EVALUATION OF EACH CANDIDATE
EVALUATE CANDIDATE #1
FOR THE 5 CRITERIA:
?8
?8
?5
?15
?10
EVALUATE CANDIDATE #2
FOR THE 5 CRITERIA:
?10
?1
?8
?10
?15
EVALUATE CANDIDATE #3
FOR THE 5 CRITERIA:
?5
?10
?8
?20
?10
```

```
** WEIGHTS OF CRITERIA
   YOU HAVE TWO OPTIONS:
   TO WEIGHT ALL CRITERIA EQUALLY,
        TYPE <1>
   TO WEIGHT THE CRITERIA DIFFERENTLY,
        TYPE <2>
   INPUT YOUR CHOICE: 2

GIVE THE WEIGHT FOR CRITERION #1 ?15
GIVE THE WEIGHT FOR CRITERION #2 ?15
GIVE THE WEIGHT FOR CRITERION #3 ?20
GIVE THE WEIGHT FOR CRITERION #4 ?30
GIVE THE WEIGHT FOR CRITERION #5 ?20

** CONCORDANCE THRESHOLD? .8
** DISCORDANCE THRESHOLD? .3

   HERE ARE THE RESULTS OF ELECTRE 1
   ---------------------------------

CONCORDANCE MATRIX? (Y/N) Y

## CONCORDANCE MATRIX
   ------------------

          A1      A2      A3

   A1     -       45      35
   A2     55      -       55
   A3     85      65      -

DISCORDANCE MATRIX? (Y/N) Y

## DISCORDANCE MATRIX
   ------------------

          A1      A2      A3

   A1     -       25      25
   A2     35      -       50
   A3     15      25      -

OUTRANKING MATRIX?  (Y/N) Y

##  OUTRANKING MATRIX
    ----------------
    ...FOR P=.8 AND Q=.3

          A1  A2  A3

   A1 ---> 0   0   0
   A2 ---> 0   0   0
   A3 ---> 1   0   0

ANOTHER ANALYSIS? (Y/N) Y

NEW CONCORDANCE THRESHOLD? .6
NEW DISCORDANCE THRESHOLD? .3

NEW WEIGHTS FOR CRITERIA? (Y/N) N
```

```
         HERE ARE THE RESULTS OF ELECTRE 1
         ---------------------------------


    CONCORDANCE MATRIX? (Y/N) N
    DISCORDANCE MATRIX? (Y/N) N
    OUTRANKING MATRIX?  (Y/N) Y

    ##   OUTRANKING MATRIX
         ------------------
       ...FOR P=.6 AND Q=.3

              A1   A2   A3

       A1 ---> 0    0    0
       A2 ---> 0    0    0
       A3 ---> 1    1    0


    ANOTHER ANALYSIS? (Y/N) N
```

The Program Listing

```
1   REM        ELECTRE 1
2   REM        BUI        1981
3   REM
4   REM        VARIABLES
5   REM        CO(I,J)  CONCORDANCE MATRIX
6   REM        DIS(I,J) DISCORDANCE MATRIX
7   REM        DO(I,J)  EVALUATION MATRIX
8   REM        EVA(I,J) GRADE POINT MATRIX
9   REM        NA       NUMBER OF CANDIDATES
10  REM        NC       NUMBER OF CRITERIA
11  REM        NK       NUMBER OF EVALUATION LEVELS
12  REM        P        CONCORDANCE THRESHOLD
13  REM        POI(I)   WEIGHT OF CRITERION I
14  REM        Q        DISCORDANCE THRESHOLD
15  REM        SUR(I,J) OUTRANKING MATRIX
16  REM
20  PRINT : PRINT : PRINT
30  PRINT "     E L E C T R E   1"
40  PRINT "     ------------------"
50  PRINT : PRINT : PRINT
60  PRINT "  ** MULTICRITERIA DECISION-AID MODEL"
70  PRINT : PRINT : PRINT
80  REM        INTERACTIVE DATA INPUT
90  INPUT "** NUMBER OF CANDIDATES? ";NA
100  IF NA < 2 THEN 90
110  DIM IDF$(NA),DIS(NA,NA),SUR(NA,NA)
120  PRINT "** NAMES OF CANDIDATES? "
125  PRINT "   (ABBREVIATE IN 3 LETTERS)"
130  FOR I = 1 TO NA: INPUT IDF$(I): NEXT I
140  PRINT
150  INPUT "** NUMBER OF CRITERIA? ";NC
160  IF NC < 2 THEN 140
```

```
170    DIM F(NC),F2(NC),POI(NC)
180    PRINT : PRINT " ** EVALUATION TABLE"
190    PRINT "    ---------- -----"
195    PRINT "    YOU HAVE TWO OPTIONS:"
200    PRINT "      - FOR A STANDARD SCALE, TYPE <1>"
210    PRINT "      - FOR YOUR OWN SCALE,   TYPE <2>"
220    INPUT "      INDICATE YOUR CHOICE: ";P1
230    IF P1 = 1 THEN 360
240    REM         NONSTANDARDIZED SCALES
250    PRINT
260    INPUT "** NUMBER OF CLASSES IN THE SCALE? ";NK
270    PRINT : PRINT "INPUT YOUR EVALUATION TABLE:"
280    DIM EVA(NK,NC)
290    PRINT
300    FOR I = 1 TO NK
310    PRINT NC;" CRITERIA FOR CLASS ";I
320    FOR J = 1 TO NC
330    INPUT EVA(I,J)
340    NEXT J,I
350    GOTO 410
360 NK = 5
370    DIM EVA(NK,NC)
380    FOR J = 1 TO NC
390    EVA(1,J) = 5:EVA(2,J) = 4
400    EVA(3,J) = 3:EVA(4,J) = 2:EVA(5,J) = 1: NEXT J
410    PRINT : PRINT "** EVALUATION OF EACH CANDIDATE"
420    FOR I = 1 TO NA
430    PRINT "EVALUATE CANDIDATE #";I
440    PRINT "FOR THE ";NC;" CRITERIA:"
450    FOR J = 1 TO NC
460    INPUT DO(I,J)
470    NEXT J,I
480    PRINT : PRINT "** WEIGHTS OF CRITERIA"
490    PRINT "    YOU HAVE TWO OPTIONS:"
500    PRINT "    TO WEIGHT ALL CRITERIA EQUALLY,"
510    PRINT "         TYPE <1>"
520    PRINT "    TO WEIGHT THE CRITERIA DIFFERENTLY, "
530    PRINT "         TYPE <2>"
540    INPUT "    INPUT YOUR CHOICE: ";P2
550    IF P2 = 1 THEN 620
560    PRINT
570    FOR I = 1 TO NC
580    PRINT "GIVE THE WEIGHT FOR CRITERION #";I;" ";
590    INPUT POI(I)
600    NEXT I
610    GOTO 630
620    FOR I = 1 TO NC:POI(I) = 1: NEXT I: PRINT
630    PRINT : INPUT "** CONCORDANCE THRESHOLD? ";P
640    INPUT "** DISCORDANCE THRESHOLD? ";Q
650    GOSUB 940
660    GOSUB 810
670    GOSUB 1180
680    GOSUB 1260
690    INPUT "ANOTHER ANALYSIS? (Y/N) ";YES$
700    IF  LEFT$ (YES$,1) = "N" THEN 800
710    PRINT
720    INPUT "NEW CONCORDANCE THRESHOLD? ";P
730    INPUT "NEW DISCORDANCE THRESHOLD? ";Q
740    PRINT : INPUT "NEW WEIGHTS FOR CRITERIA? (Y/N) ";YES$
```

```
750   IF  LEFT$ (YES$,1) = "N" THEN 670
760   INPUT "NUMBER OF WEIGHTS TO CHANGE? ";N
770   FOR K = 1 TO N: INPUT "NEW WEIGHT FOR WHICH CRITERION? ";I
780   PRINT "NEW WEIGHT FOR CRITERION #";I: INPUT POI(I): NEXT K
790   GOTO 660
800   GOTO 9999
810   REM        SUBROUTINE: CONCORDANCE DOMINANCE MATRIX
820   S1 = 0
830   FOR L = 1 TO NC:S1 = S1 + POI(L): NEXT L
840   TT = S1
850   FOR I = 1 TO NA: FOR K = 1 TO NC
860   S2 = 0
870   FOR J = 1 TO NC
880   IF DO(I,J) < DO(K,J) THEN 900
890   S2 = S2 + POI(J)
900   NEXT J
910   CO(I,K) = S2 / TT
920   NEXT K: NEXT I
930   RETURN
940   REM        SUBROUTINE: DISCORDANCE DOMINANCE MATRIX
950   FOR J = 1 TO NC
960   F(J) = EVA(1,J) - EVA(NK,J): NEXT J
970   DMA = F(1)
980   FOR J = 2 TO NC
990   IF DMA >  = F(J) THEN 1010
1000  DMA = F(J)
1010   NEXT J
1020   MM = DMA
1030   FOR I = 1 TO NA: FOR K = 1 TO NA: FOR L = 1 TO NC
1040   F2(L) = 0
1050   NEXT L
1060   FOR J = 1 TO NC
1070   IF DO(I,J) >  = DO(K,J) THEN 1090
1080   F2(J) = DO(K,J) - DO(I,J)
1090   NEXT J
1100   D2 = F2(1)
1110   FOR J = 2 TO NC
1120   IF D2 >  = F2(J) THEN 1140
1130   D2 = F2(J)
1140   NEXT J
1150   DIS(I,K) = D2 / MM
1160   NEXT K,I
1170   RETURN
1180   REM        SUBROUTINE: ZERO-ONE (OR OUTRANKING) MATRIX
1190   FOR I = 1 TO NA: FOR J = 1 TO NA
1200   SUR(I,J) = 1
1210   IF CO(I,J) >  = P AND DIS(I,J) <  = Q THEN 1230
1220   SUR(I,J) = 0
1230   NEXT J,I
1240   FOR I = 1 TO NA:SUR(I,I) = 0: NEXT I
1250   RETURN
1260   REM        SUBROUTINE: RESULTS
1270   FOR I = 1 TO 9: PRINT : NEXT I
1280   PRINT "    HERE ARE THE RESULTS OF ELECTRE 1    "
1290   PRINT " ----------------------------------    "
1300   PRINT : PRINT
1310   INPUT "CONCORDANCE MATRIX? (Y/N) ";YES$
1320   IF  LEFT$ (YES$,1) = "N" THEN 1440
1330   PRINT : PRINT "## CONCORDANCE MATRIX"
```

```
1340   PRINT "   ------------------"
1350   PRINT : FOR I = 1 TO NA: PRINT  TAB( 10);IDF$(I);"      ";: NEXT I
1360   PRINT : PRINT : FOR I = 1 TO NA: PRINT  TAB( 3);IDF$(I);"     ";
1370   FOR J = 1 TO NA
1380   C$(I,J) =  LEFT$ ( STR$ (100 * CO(I,J)),4)
1390   FOR T = 1 TO NA:C$(T,T) = " -": NEXT T
1400   X = 7 -  LEN (C$(I,J))
1410   PRINT C$(I,J);
1420   FOR T = 0 TO X: PRINT " ";: NEXT T
1430   NEXT J: PRINT : NEXT I: PRINT
1440   INPUT "DISCORDANCE MATRIX? (Y/N) ";YES$
1450   IF  LEFT$ (YES$,1) = "N" THEN 1570
1460   PRINT : PRINT "## DISCORDANCE MATRIX"
1470   PRINT "   ------------------"
1480   PRINT : FOR I = 1 TO NA: PRINT  TAB( 10);IDF$(I);"      ";: NEXT I
1490   PRINT : PRINT : FOR I = 1 TO NA: PRINT  TAB( 3);IDF$(I);"     ";
1500   FOR J = 1 TO NA
1510   C$(I,J) =  LEFT$ ( STR$ (100 * DIS(I,J)),4)
1520   FOR T = 1 TO NA:C$(T,T) = " -": NEXT T
1530   X = 7 -  LEN (C$(I,J))
1540   PRINT C$(I,J);
1550   FOR T = 0 TO X: PRINT " ";: NEXT T
1560   NEXT J: PRINT : NEXT I: PRINT
1570   INPUT "OUTRANKING MATRIX?  (Y/N) ";YES$
1580   IF  LEFT$ (YES$,1) = "N" THEN 1680
1590   PRINT : PRINT "##  OUTRANKING MATRIX"
1600   PRINT "   ----------------"
1610   PRINT "   ...FOR P=";P;" AND Q=";Q
1620   PRINT : FOR I = 1 TO NA
1630   PRINT  TAB( 11);IDF$(I);" ";: NEXT I
1640   PRINT : PRINT : FOR I = 1 TO NA
1650   PRINT  TAB( 3);IDF$(I);" ---> ";
1660   FOR J = 1 TO NA: PRINT  TAB( 6);SUR(I,J);"     ";
1670   NEXT J: PRINT : NEXT I: PRINT
1680   RETURN
9999   END
```

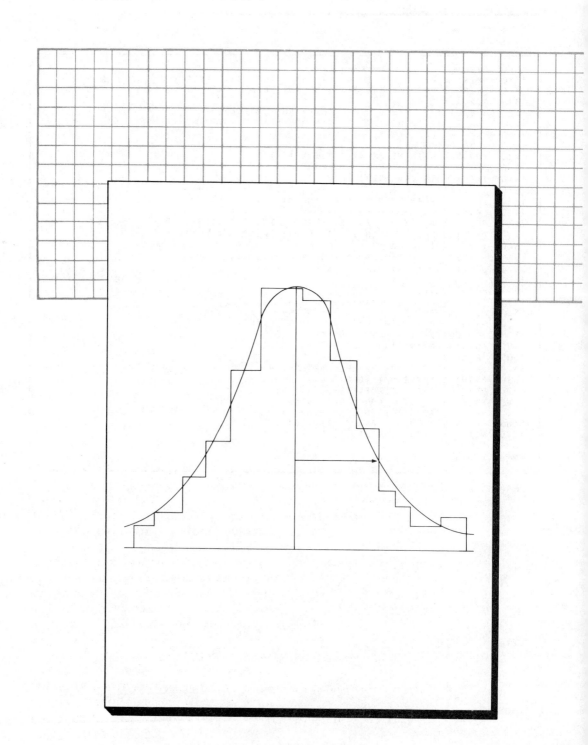

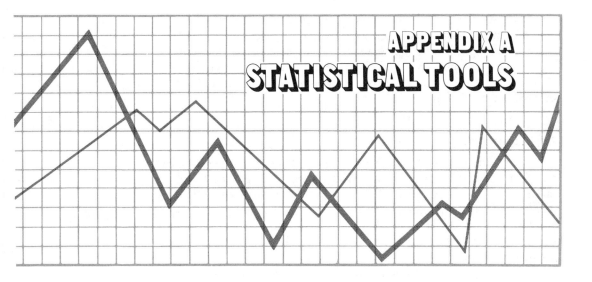

Given a set of numerical data, some form of simplification is often desirable. We may wish to clarify or classify certain characteristics of these empirical observations. From this information the analyst can construct graphs (histograms, or frequency distribution diagrams), determine central characteristics (the mean), dispersion (variance, standard deviation), and compare two or more sets of statistics (covariances, correlations).

This appendix presents three programs that will aid the analyst in implementing these statistical tools. Each of the programs is followed by an application example. The examples show not only how the programs work, but also how they can be used as aids to business decision making.

HISTOGRAMS AND NORMAL DISTRIBUTION

This program calculates frequency distributions of a set of raw data, and presents them in *graphical* form. The program integrates the *normal curve* (or Gaussian distribution) into the histogram to give a clearer picture of the statistical distribution. This program proves useful for dealing with large quantities of data that must be classified into categories.

We should note that the significance of a histogram depends essentially on the range, or amplitude, of its classifications. This interactive program allows the user to continue constructing histograms for the given data until a suitable range is found.

Application Example

A tennis club wants to open a snack bar near the courts. Ms. Novak, the manager of the club, needs to know what the members are most likely to buy from the snack bar. Starting from the hypothesis that tastes and eating habits vary according to age, Novak wants to study the distribution of ages among the members of the club. She is particularly interested in members of ages 15 to 50, since these are the people who show up at the club most often at meal times.

The program produces a histogram dividing up the age groups. The mean age is about 31, but the normal distribution curve indicates the importance of the age groups from 15 to 19 and from 20 to 24. In other words, using the mean as a reference point is only valid if the empirical distribution *follows* the normal curve.

Since the algorithm that produces the histogram uses a scaling technique to keep the graph within a certain output format, one character on the graph (*) may represent more than one observed value for some applications. The relative proportions of the elements of the graph remain significant, however.

```
┌─The Output────────────────────────────────

     HISTOGRAM AND NORMAL DISTRIBUTION
     -----------------------------------

     NUMBER OF OBSERVATIONS? 50

     * OBSERVATION #1     ?32
     * OBSERVATION #2     ?35
     * OBSERVATION #3     ?23
     * OBSERVATION #4     ?12
     * OBSERVATION #5     ?29
     * OBSERVATION #6     ?18
     * OBSERVATION #7     ?17
     * OBSERVATION #8     ?21
     * OBSERVATION #9     ?23
     * OBSERVATION #10    ?45
     * OBSERVATION #11    ?37
     * OBSERVATION #12    ?38
```

```
*  OBSERVATION #13   ?54
*  OBSERVATION #14   ?34
*  OBSERVATION #15   ?56
*  OBSERVATION #16   ?68
*  OBSERVATION #17   ?12
*  OBSERVATION #18   ?26
*  OBSERVATION #19   ?19
*  OBSERVATION #20   ?17
*  OBSERVATION #21   ?15
*  OBSERVATION #22   ?32
*  OBSERVATION #23   ?33
*  OBSERVATION #24   ?16
*  OBSERVATION #25   ?67
*  OBSERVATION #26   ?56
*  OBSERVATION #27   ?11
*  OBSERVATION #28   ?21
*  OBSERVATION #29   ?24
*  OBSERVATION #30   ?56
*  OBSERVATION #31   ?16
*  OBSERVATION #32   ?17
*  OBSERVATION #33   ?16
*  OBSERVATION #34   ?45
*  OBSERVATION #35   ?37
*  OBSERVATION #36   ?42
*  OBSERVATION #37   ?51
*  OBSERVATION #38   ?19
*  OBSERVATION #39   ?20
*  OBSERVATION #40   ?31
*  OBSERVATION #41   ?21
*  OBSERVATION #42   ?20
*  OBSERVATION #43   ?17
*  OBSERVATION #44   ?15
*  OBSERVATION #45   ?8
*  OBSERVATION #46   ?71
*  OBSERVATION #47   ?62
*  OBSERVATION #48   ?14
*  OBSERVATION #49   ?59
*  OBSERVATION #50   ?31

NUMBER OF CLASSES IN THE HISTOGRAM ? 7
RANGE OR AMPLITUDE OF EACH CLASS   ? 5
LOWER BOUND OF FIRST CLASS         ? 15

-  RANGE  -   #  NORMAL
----------------------------------------
15  ->19   12  5   : ****0******* :
20  ->24    8  5   : ****0**      :
25  ->29    2  6   : **   0       :
30  ->34    6  6   : *****0*      :
35  ->39    4  5   : ****0        :
40  ->44    1  4   : *  0         :
45  ->49    2  3   : **0          :
----------------------------------------
MEAN  = 31.18
STANDARD DEVIATION = 17.2575804

KEY:
----
'*' : DISTRIBUTION OF OBSERVED VALUES
'0' : NORMAL DISTRIBUTION
```

```
NOTICE:
-------
** 5 OBSERVATIONS BELOW THE LOWER
BOUND, AND 10 OBSERVATIONS ABOVE
THE UPPER BOUND DO NOT SHOW UP ON THE
HISTOGRAM.


NEW HISTOGRAM (Y/N) ? N
```

The Program Listing

```
10    REM         HISTOGRAM AND NORMAL DISTRIBUTION PROGRAM
15    REM         BUI       4/81
20    PRINT : PRINT : PRINT
30    PRINT "HISTOGRAM AND NORMAL DISTRIBUTION"
40    PRINT "---------------------------------"
50    PRINT : PRINT : PRINT
60    INPUT "NUMBER OF OBSERVATIONS? ";N
70    DIM X(N),HI(30),DN(30),Y(30)
80    PRINT
90    FOR I = 1 TO N
100    PRINT "* OBSERVATION #";I; TAB( 20);: INPUT X(I)
110    NEXT I
120    PRINT
130    INPUT "NUMBER OF CLASSES IN THE HISTOGRAM ? ";C
140    INPUT "RANGE OR AMPLITUDE OF EACH CLASS    ? ";EC
150    INPUT "LOWER BOUND OF FIRST CLASS          ? ";BI
160    PRINT : PRINT : PRINT
170   X1 = 0:X2 = 0:X3 = 0
180    FOR I = 1 TO N
190   X1 = X1 + X(I)
200   X2 = X2 + X(I) ^ 2
210    NEXT I
220   M = X1 / N:VA = (X2 - N * M ^ 2) / (N - 1)
230    FOR I = 1 TO C:HI(I) = 0:DN(I) = 0: NEXT I
240   X3 = BI + C * EC
250   XX = 0:YY = 0
260    FOR I = 1 TO N
270    IF X(I) < BI THEN XX = XX + 1: GOTO 310
280    IF X(I) >  = X3 THEN YY = YY + 1: GOTO 310
290   J = ((X(I) - BI) / EC) + 1
300   HI(J) = HI(J) + 1
310    NEXT I
320    GOSUB 540
330    GOSUB 610
340    PRINT "MEAN  = ";M
350    PRINT "STANDARD DEVIATION = "; SQR (VA)
360    PRINT
370    PRINT "KEY:": PRINT "----"
380    PRINT "'*' : DISTRIBUTION OF OBSERVED VALUES"
390    PRINT "'O' : NORMAL DISTRIBUTION"
400    IF XX = 0 AND YY = 0 THEN 450
```

```
410   PRINT "NOTICE:": PRINT "-------"
420   PRINT "** ";XX;" OBSERVATIONS BELOW THE LOWER "
430   PRINT "BOUND, AND ";YY;" OBSERVATIONS ABOVE"
435   PRINT "THE UPPER BOUND DO NOT SHOW UP ON THE"
440   PRINT "HISTOGRAM."
450   PRINT : PRINT : PRINT
460   INPUT "NEW HISTOGRAM (Y/N) ? ";C$
470   IF  LEFT$ (C$,1) = "N" THEN 530
480   PRINT : PRINT
490   INPUT "NEW NUMBER OF CLASSES     ? ";C
500   INPUT "NEW RANGE OF EACH CLASS   ? ";EC
510   INPUT "NEW LOWER BOUND           ? ";BI
520   GOTO 230
530   GOTO 1100
540   REM        NORMAL DISTRIBUTION SUBROUTINE
550   FOR J = 1 TO C
560   X = BI + (J * EC)
570   CU =  EXP ( - 1 * (X - M) ^ 2 / (2 * VA)) / (2.5066 *  SQR (VA))
580   DN(J) = N * EC * CU
590   NEXT J
600   RETURN
610   REM         SUBROUTINE PLOTS
620   LM = 1:LN = 0:MA = 0:MB = 0
630   FOR J = 1 TO C
640   IF HI(J) < = LN THEN 660
650   LN = HI(J)
660   NEXT J
670   FOR I = 0 TO C
680   IF HI(I) > MA GOTO 685ELSE GOTO 690
685 MA = HI(I)
690   IF DN(I) > MB THEN MB = DN(I)
700   NEXT I
710   IF LN > 45 THEN B1 = 45
720   B1 = MA:B2 = MB
730   B1 = MA / B1:B2 = MB / B2
740   LN = LN / B1:LM = LM / B2
750   REM        PRINT HISTOGRAM AND NORMAL CURVE
760   PRINT "- RANGE  -    #   NORMAL"
770   PRINT "-------------------------------------"
780   REM
790   Y(0) = BI
800   FOR J = 1 TO C
810   Y(J) = BI + (J * EC)
820   K = HI(J) * LM + .5
830   IF K < = 0 THEN 840
840   L = DN(J) * LM + .5
850   IF K > 40 THEN 1040
860   IF K < = 0 THEN 1040
870   IF L > K THEN 970
880   PRINT Y(J - 1); TAB( 5);"->";Y(J) - 1; TAB( 14);HI(J);
890   PRINT  TAB( 18); INT (DN(J) + .5); TAB( 23);": ";
900   IF HI(J) = 0 AND L < 1 THEN 1040
910   IF HI(J) = 0 AND L > 1 THEN 1030
920   FOR KK = 1 TO L - 1
930   PRINT "*";: NEXT KK
940   PRINT "0";
950   FOR KK = L + 1 TO K: PRINT "*";: NEXT KK
960   GOTO 1040
970   PRINT Y(J - 1); TAB( 5);"->";Y(J) - 1; TAB( 14);HI(J);
```

```
980    PRINT  TAB( 18); INT (DN(J) + .5); TAB( 23);": ";
990    IF HI(J) = 0 AND L < 1 THEN 1040
1000   IF HI(J) = 0 AND L > 1 THEN 1030
1010   FOR KK = 1 TO K: PRINT "*";: NEXT KK
1020   IF L = 0 THEN 1040
1030   PRINT  TAB( 23 + L);"0";
1040   PRINT  TAB( 39);":"
1050   NEXT J
1060   PRINT "--------------------------------------"
1070   RETURN
1100   END
```

MEAN, STANDARD DEVIATION, VARIANCES, COVARIANCES, CORRELATION

Given a set of historical data, this program calculates the mean, the standard deviation, the variance-covariance matrix, and the correlation matrix. The determination of the covariances between two or more sets of data is the basis of almost all econometric models.

The indices of correlation and covariance must be interpreted cautiously. When two variables have a high correlation coefficient (implying a close relationship) we must guard against assuming that there is a *causal* relationship. Both variables might, for example, be controlled by the influence of a third variable. Causality implies correlation; however, correlation *does not* necessarily imply causality.

Application Example

The sample run for this program shows one of the many possible uses for these statistical values in management. The manager of a grocery store is studying the demand for four categories of drinks: beer, wine, cola, and mineral water. The first table produced in the output shows the mean and the standard deviation for each of the four categories. The second and third tables display the variance-covariance matrix and the correlation matrix, respectively. Since these two matrices are symmetrical around their diagonals, they are most clearly presented in triangular form.

The figures show a strong correlation between mineral water and beer on the one hand, and between mineral water and cola on the other. There are *negative correlations* between wine and cola (-0.1) and between beer and wine (-0.03). These figures seem to confirm qualitative observations on the buying habits of the store's customers. Beer drinkers and wine drinkers belong to two different groups. In addition, mineral water and cola are often purchased together, while wine and cola are products that seem to substitute for each other.

```
MEAN, VARIANCE-COVARIANCE, CORRELATION
--------------------------------------


NUMBER OF VARIABLES      ? 4

NUMBER OF OBSERVATIONS   ? 5


NAME OF VARIABLE #1? BEER
NAME OF VARIABLE #2? WINE
NAME OF VARIABLE #3? COLA
NAME OF VARIABLE #4? WATER


OBSERVATIONS FOR VARIABLE 'BEER'
* VALUE FOR PERIOD 1       ?300
* VALUE FOR PERIOD 2       ?350
* VALUE FOR PERIOD 3       ?420
* VALUE FOR PERIOD 4       ?380
* VALUE FOR PERIOD 5       ?370


OBSERVATIONS FOR VARIABLE 'WINE'
* VALUE FOR PERIOD 1       ?180
* VALUE FOR PERIOD 2       ?200
* VALUE FOR PERIOD 3       ?170
* VALUE FOR PERIOD 4       ?210
* VALUE FOR PERIOD 5       ?220


OBSERVATIONS FOR VARIABLE 'COLA'
* VALUE FOR PERIOD 1       ?530
* VALUE FOR PERIOD 2       ?600
* VALUE FOR PERIOD 3       ?620
* VALUE FOR PERIOD 4       ?570
* VALUE FOR PERIOD 5       ?580


OBSERVATIONS FOR VARIABLE 'WATER'
* VALUE FOR PERIOD 1       ?440
* VALUE FOR PERIOD 2       ?570
* VALUE FOR PERIOD 3       ?580
* VALUE FOR PERIOD 4       ?540
* VALUE FOR PERIOD 5       ?550

WEIGHTED PERIOD: N    <1>
                 N-1  <2> ?2

X(I)      AVERAGE   STD. DEV.
----------------------------
BEER       364       43.93
WINE       196       20.73
COLA       580       33.91
WATER      536       55.94

CONTINUE? Y
```

```
MATRIX OF VARIANCES-COVARIANCES
-------------------------------
        BEER    WINE    COLA    WATER
BEER    1930
WINE    -30     430
COLA    1250    -75     1150
WATER   2070    230     1800    3130

CONTINUE? Y


CORRELATION MATRIX
------------------
        BEER    WINE    COLA    WATER
BEER    1
WINE    -.033   1
COLA    .839    -.1067  1
WATER   .8422   .1982   .9487   1
```

The Program Listing

```
10   REM       MEAN, VARIANCE-COVARIANCE, CORRELATION
15   REM       BUI       4/81
20   PRINT : PRINT : PRINT
30   PRINT "MEAN, VARIANCE-COVARIANCE, CORRELATION"
40   PRINT "---------------------------------------"
50   PRINT : PRINT : PRINT
60   INPUT "NUMBER OF VARIABLES     ? ";M: PRINT
70   INPUT "NUMBER OF OBSERVATIONS  ? ";N: PRINT
80   DIM X(M,N),S(M,M),R(M,M),X1(M),X$(M)
90   FOR I = 1 TO M
95   PRINT "NAME OF VARIABLE #";I;: INPUT "? ";X$(I)
100  NEXT I: PRINT
110  FOR I = 1 TO M: PRINT "OBSERVATIONS FOR VARIABLE '";X$(I);"'"
120  FOR J = 1 TO N: PRINT "* VALUE FOR PERIOD ";J; TAB( 27);
130  INPUT X(I,J): NEXT J: PRINT : NEXT I
131  PRINT "WEIGHTED PERIOD: N    <1>"
132  INPUT "               N-1  <2> ?";C
133  PRINT : PRINT
134  IF C = 1 THEN C = N: GOTO 140
135  C = N - 1
140  GOSUB 530
150  GOSUB 600
160  IF M < = 1 THEN 180
170  GOSUB 700
180  FOR I = 1 TO M
190  FOR J = I TO M
200  S(I,J) = S(I,J) / C
210  S(J,I) = S(I,J)
220  NEXT J,I
230  REM       OUTPUT SECTION
240  PRINT "X(I)"; TAB( 10);"AVERAGE"; TAB( 20);"STD. DEV."
250  PRINT "------------------------------"
260  FOR I = 1 TO M
```

```
270    PRINT X$(I); TAB( 12); INT (100 * X1(I) + .5) / 100; TAB( 22); INT (
       100 *  SQR (S(I,I))) / 100
280    NEXT I
290    IF M < = 1 THEN 250
300    PRINT
310    INPUT "CONTINUE? ";C$: PRINT : PRINT
320    PRINT "MATRIX OF VARIANCES-COVARIANCES"
330    PRINT "-----------------------------"
340    FOR I = 1 TO M: PRINT  TAB( 8 * I);X$(I);: NEXT I: PRINT
350    FOR I = 1 TO M
360    PRINT X$(I);
370    FOR J = 1 TO M
380    IF J > I THEN 400
390    PRINT  TAB( 8 * J); INT (10000 * S(I,J)) / 10000;
400    NEXT J: PRINT
410    NEXT I: PRINT
420    INPUT "CONTINUE? ";C$: PRINT : PRINT
430    PRINT "CORRELATION MATRIX"
440    PRINT "------------------"
450    FOR I = 1 TO M: PRINT  TAB( 8 * I);X$(I);: NEXT I: PRINT
460    FOR I = 1 TO M
470    PRINT X$(I);
480    FOR J = 1 TO M
490    IF J > I THEN 510
500    PRINT  TAB( 8 * J); INT (10000 * R(I,J)) / 10000;
510    NEXT J: PRINT : NEXT I
520    GOTO 800
530    REM   AVERAGE SUBROUTINE
540    FOR I = 1 TO M
550 S1 = 0
560    FOR J = 1 TO N:S1 = S1 + X(I,J): NEXT J
570    X1(I) = S1 / N
580    NEXT I
590    RETURN
600    REM       VARIANCE-COVARIANCE SUBROUTINE
610    FOR I = 1 TO M
620    FOR K = 1 TO M
630 S2 = 0
640    FOR J = 1 TO N
650 S2 = S2 + (X(I,J) - X1(I)) * (X(K,J) - X1(K))
660    NEXT J
670 S(I,K) = S2:S(K,I) = S2
680    NEXT K,I
690    RETURN
700    REM       CORRELATION SUBROUTINE
710 R(1,1) = 1
720    FOR J = 2 TO M
730 R(J,J) = 1
740 J1 = J - 1
750    FOR I = 1 TO J1
760 R(I,J) = S(I,J) /  SQR (S(I,I) * S(J,J))
770 R(J,I) = R(I,J)
780    NEXT I,J
790    RETURN
800    END
```

RANK CORRELATION

Instead of using precise values of variances (when, for example, precise measurement is impossible) we can *rank* the data in order of importance and then calculate the *rank-correlation coefficient,* often called Spearman's correlation coefficient. Given two lists of ranked values, Spearman's formula for the correlation, *r,* is:

$$r = 1 - \frac{6(\Sigma d^2)}{n(n^2 - 1)}$$

where

d = the difference between each pair of ranks
n = the number of pairs

After the input of two lists of ranked data, this program calculates the rank correlation. Spearman's formula is implemented in lines 240 to 280.

Application Example

The sample run of this program illustrates an attempt to evaluate the effect of advertising on the sales of ten popular brands of perfume. The data input for observation #1 indicates that the perfume that is first in sales ranks fourth in the amount of advertising; observation #2 shows that the second most popular perfume ranks third in advertising; and so on.

The program computes a rank correlation of 86.67%, indicating a significant relationship between advertising and sales. However, since the correlation is not perfect (i.e., 100%), we can assume that other factors must be considered when analyzing sales behavior.

The Output

```
SPEARMAN RANK CORRELATION
---------------------------


NUMBER OF OBSERVATIONS ? 10

NAME OF THE FIRST VARIABLE ? SALES

NAME OF THE SECOND VARIABLE ? ADVERTISING


OBSERVATION #1:
RANK IN SALES              ?1
RANK IN ADVERTISING        ?4
```

```
OBSERVATION #2:
RANK IN SALES                    ?2
RANK IN ADVERTISING              ?3


OBSERVATION #3:
RANK IN SALES                    ?3
RANK IN ADVERTISING              ?1


OBSERVATION #4:
RANK IN SALES                    ?4
RANK IN ADVERTISING              ?2


OBSERVATION #5:
RANK IN SALES.                   ?5
RANK IN ADVERTISING              ?5


OBSERVATION #6:
RANK IN SALES                    ?6
RANK IN ADVERTISING              ?7


OBSERVATION #7:
RANK IN SALES                    ?7
RANK IN ADVERTISING              ?6


OBSERVATION #8:
RANK IN SALES                    ?8
RANK IN ADVERTISING              ?8


OBSERVATION #9:
RANK IN SALES                    ?9
RANK IN ADVERTISING              ?10


OBSERVATION #10:
RANK IN SALES                    ?10
RANK IN ADVERTISING              ?9


-----------------------------------------
OBSERVATION    SALES    ADVERTISING

    1            1           4
    2            2           3
    3            3           1
    4            4           2
    5            5           5
    6            6           7
    7            7           6
    8            8           8
    9            9          10
   10           10           9


RANK CORRELATION = 86.67%
-----------------------------------------
```

The Program Listing

```
10   REM        RANK CORRELATION
15   REM        BUI     4/81
20   PRINT : PRINT : PRINT
30   PRINT "SPEARMAN RANK CORRELATION"
40   PRINT "-------------------------"
50   PRINT : PRINT
60   INPUT "NUMBER OF OBSERVATIONS ? ";N
70   PRINT
80   INPUT "NAME OF THE FIRST VARIABLE ? ";X$
90   PRINT
100  INPUT "NAME OF THE SECOND VARIABLE ? ";Y$
110  PRINT : PRINT
120  DIM R1(N),R2(N),R(N),S(N)
130  FOR I = 1 TO N
140  PRINT "OBSERVATION #";I;":"
150  PRINT "RANK IN ";X$; TAB( 30);
160  INPUT R1(I)
170  PRINT "RANK IN ";Y$; TAB( 30);
180  INPUT R2(I)
190  PRINT
200  NEXT I
210  REM         CALCULATION SECTION
220  REM         CALCULATE THE DIFFERENCES
230  REM          IN THE RANKS, CORRELATION
240  D2 = 0
250  FOR I = 1 TO N
260  D2 = D2 + (R1(I) - R2(I)) ^ 2
270  NEXT I
280  R1 = 1 - (6 * D2) / (N ^ 3 - N)
290  REM         PRINT INPUT DATA AND RESULTS
300  PRINT : PRINT
305  PRINT "---------------------------------------"
310  PRINT "OBSERVATION"; TAB( 15);X$; TAB( 25);Y$
320  PRINT
330  FOR I = 1 TO N
340  PRINT  TAB( 4);I; TAB( 17);R1(I); TAB( 27);R2(I)
350  NEXT I
360  PRINT : PRINT
370  PRINT "RANK CORRELATION = "; INT (10000 * R1 + .5) / 100;"%"
380  PRINT "---------------------------------------"
390  END
```

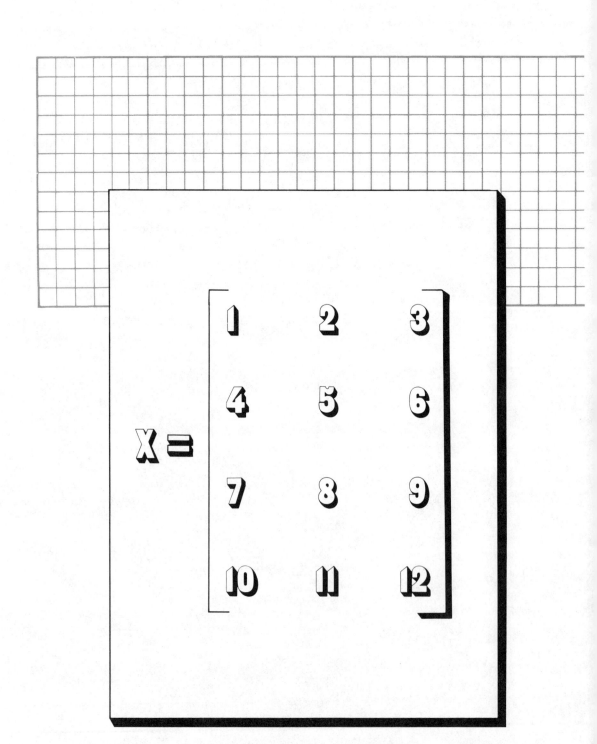

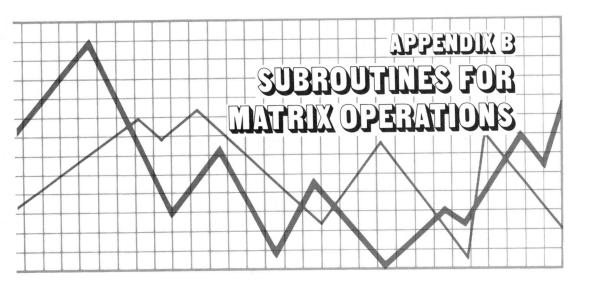

APPENDIX B
SUBROUTINES FOR
MATRIX OPERATIONS

Although some versions of BASIC supply instructions and functions for matrix arithmetic, many implementations do not have these features. This appendix presents three useful subroutines for matrix operations frequently needed in programming for business management tools.

MATRIX ADDITION AND SUBTRACTION

Given two matrices A and B of the same order (i.e., both having the same number of rows and the same number of columns) the sum of A and B is a new matrix, C, also of the same order. Each element of C is the sum of the corresponding elements of A and B:

```
100 REM MATRIX ADDITION
110 FOR I = 1 TO M
120     FOR J = 1 TO N
130         C(I,J) = A(I,J) + B(I,J)
140     NEXT J
150 NEXT I
```

For matrix subtraction, simply replace line 130 with the following line:

130    $C(I,J) = A(I,J) - B(I,J)$

MATRIX MULTIPLICATION

Given two matrices A and B, the product AB can be calculated if and only if the number of columns in matrix A is equal to the number of rows in matrix B. The order of the multiplication is important: the product AB is not, in general, equal to the product BA; that is to say, matrix multiplication is not commutative.

If A is a matrix of m rows by p columns, and B is a matrix of p rows by n columns, then their product, C, will be a matrix of m rows by n columns. The element c_{ij} of the matrix C is calculated by multiplying the elements of the ith row of A by the corresponding elements of the jth column of B and adding the results:

$$C_{ij} = \sum_{k=1}^{p} a_{ik} b_{kj}$$

where:

$$i = 1, 2, \ldots, m$$
$$j = 1, 2, \ldots, n$$
$$k = 1, 2, \ldots, p$$

```
100 REM MATRIX MULTIPLICATION
110 FOR I = 1 TO M
120    FOR J = 1 TO N
130        C(I,J) = 0 : REM INITIALIZE EACH ELEMENT OF C
140        FOR K = 1 TO P
150            C(I,J) = C(I,J) + A(I,K) * B(K,J)
160        NEXT K
170    NEXT J
180 NEXT I
```

INVERSION OF A SQUARE MATRIX

Given a nonsingular square matrix A of order n, we determine its *inverse*, A^{-1}, as a square matrix of order n such that:

$$A A^{-1} = I$$

where I is the *unit matrix*. Note that a *nonsingular* matrix is one whose determinant is not equal to zero. A unit matrix has values of 1 along its *principal diagonal* and values of 0 elsewhere; for example:

$$\begin{bmatrix} 1 & 0 & 0 \\ 0 & 1 & 0 \\ 0 & 0 & 1 \end{bmatrix}$$

Note also that if A^{-1} exists, it is unique; that is, at most one inverse matrix exists for every square matrix.

```
100 REM MATRIX INVERSION
110 FOR L = 1 TO N
120    X = A(L,L)
130    IF X <> 0 THEN 150
140    PRINT "SINGULAR MATRIX" : STOP
150    A(L,L) = 1
160    FOR J = 1 TO N
170       A(L,J) = A(L,J)/X
180    NEXT J
190    FOR I = 1 TO N
200       IF I = L THEN 260
210       X = A(I,L)
220       A(I,L) = 0
230       FOR J = 1 TO N
240          A(I,J) = A(I,J) − X * A(L,J)
250       NEXT J
260    NEXT I
270 NEXT L
```

```
540  FOR M=1 TO G
550  IF S(M)<=T THEN580
560  NEXT M
570  GOTO670
580  IF B=E THEN670
590  B= B+1
600  S(M) = C(FNA(B),2)+T
610  K(M)=K(M)+1
620  REM T1: temps d'att
630  T1= T - C(FNA(B)
640  REM T2: temp--
650  T2= T2 + ¯
660  GOTO530
670  REM st
680  L= E-
690  L1=I
700  F¯
710
7¯
¯
```

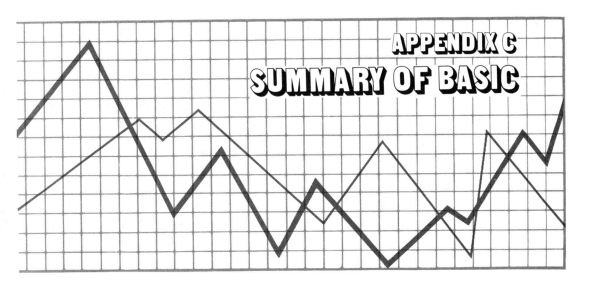

Note: This summary covers the elements of BASIC that are used in the programs in this book.

THE RESERVED WORDS

INSTRUCTION	EXAMPLE	EXPLANATION
DEF FN	40 **DEF FN**A(X)=2*X	User-defined function.
DIM	30 **DIM** A(12), B(5,5)	Reserves memory space for an array (or arrays) of the specified length and dimension.
END	999 **END**	Designates the end of a program, and terminates execution. (Optional)

FOR/NEXT	10 **FOR** X=1 **TO** 10 **STEP** 2 20 ... 30 **NEXT** X	Permits repetition of the group of instructions placed between the **FOR** line and the **NEXT** line. The number of iterations is determined by the initial values of **FOR** and by the **STEP**. The **STEP** instruction is only needed if the steps of progression are different from 1.
GOSUB/RETURN	100 **GOSUB** 500 500 ... 600 **RETURN**	Transfers control of the program to a subroutine and permits return of control to the main program.
GOTO	45 **GOTO** 90	Transfers control of the program to the specified line number.
IF/THEN	10 **IF** X=5 **THEN** 50 20 **IF** X=7 **THEN PRINT** X	Permits execution of a conditional instruction following the evaluation of a logical expression. If the expression is false the statement after **THEN** is ignored and control passes to the following line of the program; if true, then the statement after **THEN** is executed.
IF/GOTO	30 **IF** X=5 **GOTO** 50 40 **IF** X=5 **THEN** 50	Lines 30 and 40 are identical.
INPUT	40 **INPUT** X 70 **INPUT** "PRICE"; X	Permits introduction of string or numerical values from the keyboard during the execution of program.
LET	20 **LET** A = (C−B) * 2	Assigns a value to a variable. (The word **LET** is optional in many BASICs).
NEXT	See **FOR/NEXT**	Ends a loop that was begun by a **FOR** statement.

ON/GOTO	10 **ON** X **GOTO** 20,30,40	Control skips to the specified line according to the value of X: If X = 1, to line 20 X = 2, to line 30 X = 3, to line 40 If the value of X falls outside of the appropriate range, the results depend on the version of BASIC being used.
PRINT	80 **PRINT** X 90 **PRINT** "PRICE #"; X	Prints the contents of the list of expressions, variables, or results.
RANDOMIZE	10 **RANDOMIZE**	Initializes the "seed" of the random number generator; assures an unpredictable sequence of random numbers each time the random number generator is used. For some versions of BASIC, this instruction should be replaced by: Z = **RND**(−1)
REM	10 **REM** TEST PROGRAM	Declares the lines that follow as a remark, or comment; useful for documentation of program.
RETURN	See **GOSUB/RETURN**	Returns control of program to the line following the **GOSUB** statement.

NUMERIC FUNCTIONS

FUNCTION	EXAMPLE	EXPLANATION
ABS(X)	20 Y = **ABS**(X)	Returns the absolute value of X.

EXP(X)	10 Y = **EXP**(3.45)	Computes e^x where e = 2.71828.
INT(X)	40 Y = **INT**(2.72)	Truncates X.
RND(X)	70 Y=(B−A)∗RND(0)+A	Generates a random number. (Note: the argument of **RND** and the range of the numbers it generates are implementation dependent.)
SGN(X)	20 Y = **SGN**(X)	Returns a 1 if the value of X is positive, a −1 if the value of X is negative, and a 0 if X equals 0.
SQR(X)	80 Y = **SQR**(X)	Finds the square root of X.
TAB(X)	60 PRINT **TAB**(15);X	Tabs to the specified column.
LOG(X)	50 Y = **LOG**(235)	Returns the natural logarithm (i.e., to the base e). To find log$_{10}$ use the following formula: **LOG**(X)/**LOG**(10)

STRING FUNCTIONS

FUNCTION	EXAMPLE	EXPLANATION
LEN(X$)	10 X$="PRICE" 20 **PRINT LEN**(X$)	Gives the length of the string X$.
**LEFT$**(X$,I)	10 C$ = "YES" 20 **PRINT LEFT$**(C$,1)	Returns the first I characters of the string X$.
**RIGHT$**(X$,I)	10 C$="10549ML" 20 **PRINT RIGHT$**(C$,2)	Returns the last I characters of the string X$.
STR$(X)	10 C$ = **STR$**(X)	Converts the numeric value X into a string.

ARITHMETIC OPERATIONS

SYMBOL	EXAMPLE	EXPLANATION
=	10 A = 1250.5	Assignment
−	30 C = −B	Arithmetic negation
∧	20 Y = X∧4	Exponentiation
*	50 C = A*B	Multiplication
/	90 D = L/M	Division
+	80 E = L + M	Addition
−	70 F = L − M	Subtraction

LOGICAL OPERATORS

SYMBOL	EXAMPLE	EXPLANATION
=	10 **IF** A=10 **THEN PRINT** A	Equality
<>	20 **IF** A<>10 **GOTO** 900	Inequality
>	30 **IF** B>A **GOTO** 888	Greater than
<	40 **IF** A<B **GOTO** 700	Less than
>=	50 **IF** A>=C **GOTO** 500	Greater than or equal to
<=	60 **IF** A<=C **GOTO** 550	Less than or equal to
AND	70 **IF** B<A **AND** A<C **GOTO** 5	Logical intersection
OR	80 **IF** B>A **OR** A>C **THEN** 5	Logical union
NOT	90 **IF NOT** B>C **THEN** 90	Logical negation

ORDER OF OPERATIONS

Operations are executed in the following order:

1. function call **FN**
2. parentheses ( )
3. exponentiation ^
4. sign change −
5. multiplication and * / division (left to right)
6. addition and + − subtraction (left to right)

BIBLIOGRAPHY

OPERATIONS RESEARCH AND MANAGEMENT SCIENCE

Brown, Kenneth, and Revelle, Jack. *Quantitative Methods for Managerial Decisions.* Reading, Mass.: Addison-Wesley Publishing Company, 1978.

Hillier, Frederick S., and Lieberman, Gerald J. *Introduction to Operations Research.* San Francisco: Holden-Day, Inc., 1980.

Horngren, Charles T. *Introduction to Management Accounting.* Fourth Edition. Englewood Cliffs: Prentice-Hall, Inc., 1978.

Shore, Barry. *Quantitative Methods for Business Decisions: Text and Cases.* New York: McGraw-Hill Book Company, 1978.

Thompson, Gerald E. *Management Science: An Introduction to Modern Quantitative Analysis and Decision Making.* New York: McGraw-Hill Book Company, 1976.

BUSINESS STATISTICS

Brandt, Siegmund. *Statistical Methods in Data Analysis.* Revised Edition. New York: North Holland Publishing Company, 1976.

Chance, William. *Statistical Methods for Decision Making.* Homewood, Illinois: Richard D. Irwin, Inc., 1969.

Freund, John E., and Williams, Frank J. *Elementary Business Statistics: the Modern Approach.* Third Edition. Englewood Cliffs: Prentice-Hall, Inc. 1977.

Spirer, Herbert F. *Business Statistics: A Problem Solving Approach.* Homewood, Illinois: Richard D. Irwin, Inc., 1975.

FINANCIAL AND PORTFOLIO MANAGEMENT

Ahlers, David M., and Cohen, Kalman J. *A New Look at Portfolio Management.* Greenwich, Connecticut: JAI Press, 1977.

Elton, Edwin, and Gruber, Martin. *Modern Portfolio Theory and Investment Analysis.* New York: John Wiley & Sons, 1981.

Weston, Fred, and Brigham, Eugene. *Managerial Finance.* Sixth Edition. Hinsdale, Illinois: The Dryen Press, 1978.

INDEX

The SYBEX Library

BASIC PROGRAMS FOR SCIENTISTS AND ENGINEERS
by **Alan R. Miller**   340 pp., 120 illustr., Ref. B240
This second book in the "Programs for Scientists and Engineers" series provides a library of problem solving programs while developing proficiency in BASIC.

INSIDE BASIC GAMES
by **Richard Mateosian**   350 pp., 240 Illustr., Ref. B245
Teaches interactive BASIC programming through games. Games are written in Microsoft BASIC and can run on the TRS-80, APPLE II and PET/CBM.

FIFTY BASIC EXERCISES
by **J.P. Lamoitier**   240 pp., 195 Illustr., Ref. B250
Teaches BASIC by actual practice using graduated exercises drawn from everyday applications. All programs written in Microsoft BASIC.

EXECUTIVE PLANNING WITH BASIC
by **X.T. Bui**   192 pp., 19 illustr., Ref. B380
An important collection of business management decision models in BASIC, including Inventory Management (EOQ), Critical Path Analysis and PERT, Financial Ratio Analysis, Portfolio Management, and much more.

BASIC FOR BUSINESS
by **Douglas Hergert**   250 pp., 15 illustr., Ref. B390
A logically organized, no-nonsense introduction to BASIC programming for business applications. Includes many fully explained accounting programs, and shows you how to write them.

YOUR FIRST COMPUTER
by **Rodnay Zaks**   260 pp., 150 Illustr., Ref. C200A
The most popular introduction to small computers and their peripherals: what they do and how to buy one.

DON'T (or How to Care for Your Computer)
by **Rodnay Zaks**   220 pp., 100 Illustr., Ref. C400
The correct way to handle and care for all elements of a computer system including what to do when something doesn't work.

INTRODUCTION TO WORD PROCESSING
by **Hal Glatzer**   200 pp., 70 illustr., Ref. W101
Explains in plain language what a word processor can do, how it improves productivity, how to use a word processor and how to buy one wisely.

INTRODUCTION TO WORDSTAR
by **Arthur Naiman**   200 pp., 30 illustr., Ref. W110
Makes it easy to learn how to use WordStar, a powerful word processing program for personal computers.

FROM CHIPS TO SYSTEMS: AN INTRODUCTION TO MICROPROCESSORS
by Rodnay Zaks   560 pp., 255 illustr., Ref. C207A
A simple and comprehensive introduction to microprocessors from both a hardware and software standpoint: what they are, how they operate, how to assemble them into a complete system.

MICROPROCESSOR INTERFACING TECHNIQUES
by Rodnay Zaks and Austin Lesea   460 pp., 400 Illustr., Ref. C207
Complete hardware and software interconnect techniques including D to A conversion, peripherals, standard buses and troubleshooting.

PROGRAMMING THE 6502
by Rodnay Zaks   390 pp., 160 Illustr., Ref. C202
Assembly language programming for the 6502, from basic concepts to advanced data structures.

6502 APPLICATIONS BOOK
by Rodnay Zaks   280 pp., 205 Illustr., Ref. D302
Real life application techniques: the input/output book for the 6502.

6502 GAMES
by Rodnay Zaks   300 pp., 140 Illustr., Ref. G402
Third in the 6502 series. Teaches more advanced programming techniques, using games as a framework for learning.

PROGRAMMING THE Z80
by Rodnay Zaks   620 pp., 200 Illustr., Ref. C280
A complete course in programming the Z80 microprocessor and a thorough introduction to assembly language.

PROGRAMMING THE Z8000
by Richard Mateosian   300 pp., 125 Illustr., Ref. C281
How to program the Z8000 16-bit microprocessor. Includes a description of the architecture and function of the Z8000 and its family of support chips.

THE CP/M HANDBOOK (with MP/M)
by Rodnay Zaks   330 pp., 100 Illustr., Ref. C300
An indispensable reference and guide to CP/M—the most widely used operating system for small computers.

INTRODUCTION TO PASCAL (Including UCSD PASCAL)
by Rodnay Zaks   420 pp., 130 Illustr., Ref. P310
A step-by-step introduction for anyone wanting to learn the Pascal language. Describes UCSD and Standard Pascals. No technical background is assumed.

THE PASCAL HANDBOOK
by Jacques Tiberghien   490 pp., 350 Illustr., Ref. P320
A dictionary of the Pascal language, defining every reserved word, operator, procedure and function found in all major versions of Pascal.

PASCAL PROGRAMS FOR SCIENTISTS AND ENGINEERS
by Alan Miller   400 pp., 80 Illustr., Ref. P340
A comprehensive collection of frequently used algorithms for scientific and technical applications, programmed in Pascal. Includes such programs as curve-fitting, integrals and statistical techniques.

APPLE PASCAL GAMES
by Douglas Hergert and Joseph T. Kalash   380 pp., 40 illustr., Ref. P360
A collection of the most popular computer games in Pascal challenging the reader not only to play but to investigate how games are implemented on the computer.

INTRODUCTION TO UCSD PASCAL SYSTEMS
by Charles T. Grant and Jon Butah   300 pp., 110 illustr., Ref. P370
A simple, clear introduction to the UCSD Pascal Operating System for beginners through experienced programmers.

INTERNATIONAL MICROCOMPUTER DICTIONARY
140 pp., Ref. X2
All the definitions and acronyms of microcomputer jargon defined in a handy pocket-size edition. Includes translations of the most popular terms into ten languages.

MICROPROGRAMMED APL IMPLEMENTATION
by Rodnay Zaks   350 pp., Ref. Z10
An expert-level text presenting the complete conceptual analysis and design of an APL interpreter, and actual listings of the microcode.

SELF STUDY COURSES

Recorded live at seminars given by recognized professionals in the microprocessor field.

INTRODUCTORY SHORT COURSES:
Each includes two cassettes plus special coordinated workbook (2½ hours).

S10—INTRODUCTION TO PERSONAL AND BUSINESS COMPUTING
A comprehensive introduction to small computer systems for those planning to use or buy one, including peripherals and pitfalls.

S1—INTRODUCTION TO MICROPROCESSORS
How microprocessors work, including basic concepts, applications, advantages and disadvantages.

S2—PROGRAMMING MICROPROCESSORS
The companion to S1. How to program any standard microprocessor, and how it operates internally. Requires a basic understanding of microprocessors.

S3—DESIGNING A MICROPROCESSOR SYSTEM
Learn how to interconnect a complete system, wire by wire. Techniques discussed are applicable to all standard microprocessors.

INTRODUCTORY COMPREHENSIVE COURSES:
Each includes a 300-500 page seminar book and seven or eight C90 cassettes.

SB1—MICROPROCESSORS
This seminar teaches all aspects of microprocessors: from the operation of an MPU to the complete interconnect of a system. The basic hardware course (12 hours).

SB2—MICROPROCESSOR PROGRAMMING

The basic software course: step by step through all the important aspects of micro-computer programming (10 hours).

ADVANCED COURSES:

Each includes a 300-500 page workbook and three or four C90 cassettes.

SB3—SEVERE ENVIRONMENT/MILITARY MICROPROCESSOR SYSTEMS

Complete discussion of constraints, techniques and systems for severe environ-ment applications, including Hughes, Raytheon, Actron and other militarized systems (6 hours).

SB5—BIT-SLICE

Learn how to build a complete system with bit slices. Also examines innovative applications of bit slice techniques (6 hours).

SB6—INDUSTRIAL MICROPROCESSOR SYSTEMS

Seminar examines actual industrial hardware and software techniques, compo-nents, programs and cost (4½ hours).

SB7—MICROPROCESSOR INTERFACING

Explains how to assemble, interface and interconnect a system (6 hours).

SOFTWARE

BAS 65™ CROSS-ASSEMBLER IN BASIC

8" diskette, Ref. BAS 65
A complete assembler for the 6502, written in standard Microsoft BASIC under CP/M®.

8080 SIMULATORS

Turns any 6502 into an 8080. Two versions are available for APPLE II.

APPLE II cassette, Ref. S6580-APL(T)
APPLE II diskette, Ref. S6580-APL(D)

FOR A COMPLETE CATALOG
OF OUR PUBLICATIONS

U.S.A
2344 Sixth Street
Berkeley,
California 94710
Tel: (415) 848-8233
Telex: 336311

SYBEX-EUROPE
4 Place Félix Eboué
75583 Paris Cedex 12
Tel: 1/347-30-20
Telex: 211801

SYBEX-VERLAG
Heyestr. 22
4000 Düsseldorf 12
West Germany
Tel: (0211) 287066
Telex: 08 588 163